# Begin with the Brain

Orchestrating the Learner-Centered Classroom

Martha Kaufeldt

Zephyr
Press ®
REACHING THEIR HIGHEST POTENTIAL
Tucson, Arizona

Begin with the Brain
Orchestrating the Learner-Centered Classroom

Grades: K through 8

© 1999 by Zephyr Press
Printed in the United States of America

ISBN 1-56976-098-5

Editing: Veronica Durie and Stacey Shropshire
Cover design: Daniel Miedaner
Design and production: Daniel Miedaner
Illustrations: Mike Erickson
Promotional illustration: Trinidad Castro

Zephyr Press
P.O. Box 66006
Tucson, AZ 85728-6006
1-800-232-2187
http://www.zephyrpress.com

Library of Congress Cataloging-in-Publication Data
Kaufeldt, Martha, 1954-
    Begin with the brain : orchestrating the learner-centered
classroom  /  Martha Kaufeldt.
        p.    cm.
    Includes bibliographical references.
    ISBN 1-56976-098-5
    1. Learning, Psychology of.   2. Learning--Physiological aspects.
3. Brain.   4. Classroom environment.   I. Title.
LB1057. K38   1999
370.15'23--dc21                                            99-22436

To the boys from whom
I have learned the most:
Barney, Kurt, Kris, and Dad.
And to Mum.

# Contents

# Preface

"Don't smile until Christmas!" a master teacher told me in the mid 1970s. "Show 'em who's boss and don't back down . . . otherwise you'll lose control and it'll all be over."

Oh, brother.

I am a veteran teacher, having taught at all grade levels. I began my readings and research on the brain and learning theory in 1980 and have been applying brain-based learning concepts in my classrooms ever since. I *know* that there are a variety of ways that educators can organize their classrooms that will make them effective, productive, and most of all, *joyous* places for learning to take place. My first suggestion is to *smile.*

I've always done the best I could with what I knew at the time. I remember a year early in my career when I had thirty-eight students in a fourth- and fifth-grade class. They were creative, energetic, silly, devious, wired, curious, and fun. In 180 days I was supposed to teach them all subjects. I had to use every strategy I could think of to keep us on track. I approached it as I have at various other times in my teaching career: by giving points and time outs, by taking away privileges, personal property, and rights. I controlled and dictated, mandated and glared. I used stopwatches, stickers, tickets, and "bucks." Most of the strategies were for a good reason at the time, and many of them seemed to work for a while. Many were just desperate attempts to control the chaos.

When I finally began investigating the current research about the brain and learning, I found out that I was able to understand many of the possible reasons for my students' actions and behaviors. Once I understood the theory, I could create systems that would likely prevent the situations that kept students from being as successful as they could be.

Unfortunately, effective classroom management systems and discipline plans are not often included in credential-giving programs for beginning teachers. Even now a management class might be offered only as an elective and will most likely be based on traditional models. So new teachers are forced to look furtively at their colleagues (often the veteran teachers) to see what tricks, gimmicks, and systems they have created to keep kids on track and to keep general order in the classroom. Occasionally veteran teachers also find that during some years they seem to have a group of children in their class that are so rambunctious or downright ill-mannered that one would wonder if they were all born during a

MY FIRST SUGGESTION IS TO *SMILE.*

year with bad water. These teachers also begin to look to others for successful strategies to discover some fresh ideas for an overwhelming problem.

This book is designed to be like the teacher down the hall from whom you can get a lot of ideas for orchestrating and maintaining a harmonious classroom that is a joyous and yet rigorous place to be, a place where students understand the standards and procedures and are considered a part of the team. A classroom where every system and strategy have been thought through with how the brain works in mind. As you read this book, you will see that I don't throw out all of the incentive systems or management strategies; occasionally some of the more tried-and-true ones were intuitively based on common sense about how the brain works.

Throughout this book, I refer frequently to Monarch Community School. It was during my tenure at that school that I learned, applied, tested, improved, and tweaked many of the tools I explore in this book.

I have always been enthusiastic about creating integrated, thematic, experiential curriculum. For more than fifteen years, my year-long themes have been elaborate, complex, and challenging for my students. The active processing and instructional strategies that I incorporate demand that students be engaged, self-directed, motivated, and organized. With the brain research to support my selection of topics, I was able to design and facilitate relevant, real-world, meaningful learning experiences for my students.

Most of all I learned that the most dynamic brain-compatible unit, curriculum, or lesson delivered in a brain-antagonistic, stressful environment goes nowhere. What a waste of an incredible amount of teacher energy and effort, and of a terrific opportunity for students if you cannot take advantage of the powerful curriculum. A brain-compatible environment and teacher attitude must precede brain-compatible curriculum implementation.

We must begin to shift our thinking and strategies about classroom management and organization to reflect what we know about how the brain responds to its environment and situation.

THIS BOOK IS DESIGNED TO BE LIKE THE TEACHER DOWN THE HALL FROM WHOM YOU CAN GET A LOT OF IDEAS.

This new kind of brain-compatible classroom can occur only when the teacher understands how the brain functions, learns, and reacts to stress and fear. When educators and administrators become brain experts and can create brain-compatible learning environments, then ineffective discipline strategies and systems may eventually become obsolete.

As I wrote this book I was overwhelmed by the realization of how as a teacher I have synthesized information and ideas from such a wide variety of people and sources. Throughout my career, I have had incredible associations and wonderful opportunities to work with gifted educators and researchers. As I attempted to compile and publish my strategies for success in the classroom, I was able to reflect on the various workshops, trainings, collaborations, and mentors from whom I have benefited.

In the area of brain research and learning theory, the following people have been instrumental in influencing me through their writings and in many cases their personal connections: Thomas Armstrong, Tony Buzan, Geoffrey and Renate Caine, Mihaly Csikszentmihalyi, Linda Darling-Hammond, Marion Diamond, David Elkind, Howard Gardner, Jeanne Gibbs, William Glasser, Daniel Goleman, Leslie Hart, Jane Healy, Eric Jensen, Alfie Kohn, Joseph LeDoux, Larry Lowery, Jane Nelsen, Candace Pert, Frank Smith, Robert Sylwester, Pat Wolfe, and Harry Wong.

There are also a few personal mentors with whom I worked for many years who introduced me to innovations, invited me to work side by side with them, collaborated with me on new ideas and often challenged me with new projects: Pat Belvel, John Butts, and Susan Kovalik.

There is nearly a score of colleagues and friends who have been mentors and associates on a wide variety of projects: Trinidad Castro, MaryAnn Clare, Donna Cohick, Jenni Holly DeAmaral, Ardeth DeVries, Sarah Gonzales, Buzz Gray, Kris Kennedy, Jerry Kent, Laurie Marcellin, Jacque Melin, Barbara Pedersen, Pauline Ross (my first master teacher!), Nelda Schultz, Dave Schumaker, and Marsha Speck. Robert Ellingsen, my dear friend and partner teacher at Monarch School, deserves special recognition as a collaborator, sounding board, innovator, tireless cohort, and absolutely dedicated educator!

New inspiration has also come to me recently as I have grown to know Jeff Caplan, Jim Grant, Sandy Lydon, Jane Meade-Roberts, Matt Mordus, Nancy Nagel, Susie Phanton, Tom Takano, and Patrice Vecchione.

I am especially grateful to the FOM (Friends of Martha) who gathered over a few glasses of wine one Sunday evening to critique as well as offer supportive encouragement to me when I most needed it! Michele, Jeff, Trudy, Susie, Lisa, Kris, and Robert.

This book would not have become what it is without the vision of Joey Tanner, publisher at Zephyr Press, and the constant support, assistance, and encouragement of Veronica Durie, the managing editor. Abundant thanks to Stacey Shropshire for her editing.

*The solution . . . is for teachers to begin by harmonizing with the barriers of students. When we respect their current views and provide them with the appropriate degree of safety and opportunity to creatively explore, then we can take them beyond their immediate limitations. That is the nature of the challenge that good teachers provide.*

**—Renate and Geoffrey Caine,**
*Making Connections,* **81**

# 1
# From Fear to Flow
*Interpreting Brain Research*

## Begin with the Brain

⟩⟩ *The brain's capabilities are minimized when it encounters*
⟨⟨ *perceived threats in the environment.*

The most recent brain research confirms that perceived threat and stress in the environment inhibit the brain and minimize its capabilities. If the brain must deal with frustration, fear, or confusion, its performance is inhibited, which results in students' feeling helpless. Conversely, challenges and some degree of pressure enhance the brain's potential. Each individual is unique and will respond to challenge or threat in a unique way, but generally, humans are able to engage in optimal experiences in environments where there is a balance between challenge and low threat.

# Latest Brain Research

Over the last fifteen years educators have begun to rethink the structures of schools and the way in which curriculum is designed and implemented. A big influence on the restructuring efforts is the results of brain research that are available to us. We know that students can learn more if the curriculum is connected to their world outside school. We understand the importance of experiential learning and developmental stages. With greater understanding of the multiple intelligences, we are able to design a wide variety of instructional strategies and new assessment approaches. But even when our curricula are incredibly well designed and integrated thematically, if they are implemented in a brain-antagonistic setting, they are doomed to failure.

The classroom climate and environment must be conducive to learning. A classroom that is physically uncomfortable or maintains a threatening atmosphere or tone will minimize students' brains' ability to function at their highest potential. Understanding some of the latest research about how our brain reacts to stress and fear can help teachers know what *not* to do and begin to know what *to* do.

THE BRAIN RESPONDS TO FEAR WITH DEFENSIVE BEHAVIORS TO MAXIMIZE THE POSSIBILITY OF SURVIVING DANGEROUS SITUATIONS IN THE MOST BENEFICIAL WAY.

# Identifying Triggers of Defensive Behaviors

The brain responds to fear with defensive behaviors to maximize the possibility of surviving dangerous situations in the most beneficial way. The brain's attentional system is wired to be alert to patterns and signs in the environment that may indicate danger and threat. Not only does the brain respond to dangers that our ancestors experienced, such as quick movements, loud sounds, bright lights, and predators, but each brain also has a unique set of past experiences. These personal memories of traumatic circumstances sometimes intrude into our everyday life. We filter our present situations through such memories, which often biases our interpretation.

In our classrooms, we often see students react to situations based on their prior experiences. If we look, act, or speak like an adult with whom a student has had a fearful experience, then he might assume we will mistreat him as did that individual. If a student has had problems with the writing process, she may confuse new writing tasks with prior failures. Of course the difficulty here is that every human has a unique set of experiences, so a situation that one person might perceive as threatening will not necessarily threaten another.

When the brain perceives threat in the environment, or feels stressed, anxious, or out of control, it sends messages through the nervous system to the body and regulates the various organs to try to match the demands of the situation at hand. This adrenaline surge can occur whether our body faces physical, environmental, or emotional danger, or academic confusion and frustration. An upset stomach, a racing heart, high blood pressure, clammy hands, and a dry mouth are all signs of fear in humans.

## Reflexive and Reflective

For more than two decades, this phenomenon has been referred to as "downshifting." This term grew out of Paul MacLean's triune brain theory and is meant to suggest that, when under a perceived threat, the human brain gears up the brain stem to react to the danger at the expense of other areas of the brain. However, recent neurologic research has proved that the triune brain theory is simplistic at best and erroneous at worst. Robert Sylwester (1998), a well-known author, university professor, and synthesizer of brain research, suggests that this metaphor doesn't fully represent how our brain's complex response systems really work. Sylwester proposes that we use the terms *reflexive* and *reflective* to describe the two separate response systems in the brain.

Sylwester notes that, as the information from our senses comes into the brain, it does an instantaneous and crude evaluation of the input. It quickly compares what is being perceived in the context of prior memories and experiences that it has on file. Our body responds *reflexively* to the possible alarm, whether it is a physical threat, emotional stress, environmental danger, or academic confusion and frustration. If the sensory input either matches a negative memory or is an unknown and does not compute with any prior experiences, then the brain sounds off the 911 alert. This alert sparks the brain to produce a survival response and triggers an immediate adrenaline reaction. The brain gets the body ready to execute a possible defense: heart rhythms and blood pressure increase, stress hormones are released into the bloodstream, perspiration begins.

The sensory information about the perceived danger or threat also travels, often simultaneously, to the cortex for a more rational evaluation. When the cortex considers the situation, it might confirm that the situation is threatening, that indeed, there is a reason to react. But if this more thoughtful *reflection* suggests that we have overreacted, the brain may send out a message to counteract the reflexive message. It can turn off the adrenaline push and call off the drill. It releases the appropriate hormones to counteract the adrenal surge.

> IF THE SENSORY INPUT EITHER MATCHES A NEGATIVE MEMORY OR IS AN UNKNOWN AND DOES NOT COMPUTE WITH ANY PRIOR EXPERIENCES, THEN THE BRAIN SOUNDS OFF THE *911* ALERT.

## Shifting from Reaction to Action

The reaction phenomenon often narrows our focus to survival only, what I refer to as "going into 911 mode." This fast stress-driven system activates early programmed methods of dealing with danger or perceived threats: hitting, screaming, running, crying, hiding, and so on. But as Sylwester points out, the reflexive behaviors should not be viewed as necessarily negative. We have reflexive behaviors that are positive responses. When we react quickly—reaching to catch the glass as it tips over, slamming on the brakes for the animal in the road, getting pumped up to run a race—we are using primitive responses and programmed behaviors as appropriate responses to the conditions.

Eric Jensen (1996) provides a worthy update about the brain's reaction to stress: "The brain wants to make sure that when the negative stress is strong, creativity is set aside in favor of the faster, easy-to-implement rote, tried-and-true behaviors which may help you survive. As a result, under moderate to strong stress or threat, you'll get very constricted, predictable behaviors" (23). When a reflexive response occurs because of exposure to a perceived threat, true danger, or stress, most human brains are less capable of doing any of the following:

*being creative*

*seeing or hearing environmental clues*

*remembering and accessing prior learning*

*engaging in complex tasks, open-ended thinking, and questioning*

*sorting to filter out unimportant data*

*planning and mentally rehearsing*

*detecting patterns*

*communicating effectively*

*engaging in complex intellectual tasks*

I recall that as I used my old computer, I would often run out of accessible memory (RAM). I would get a message on the screen that said I needed to close some applications or windows before I could open new applications. I simply could not do everything at once and my computer demanded that I use and keep open only the windows that were absolutely necessary. In effect, the same thing often goes on in the brain when it reacts to a perceived threat; other windows and applications will be temporarily closed so that the available RAM can be devoted to the defense reflex.

STUDIES SHOW CHRONIC STRESS CAN RESULT IN A DEPRESSED IMMUNE SYSTEM, WHICH CAN CAUSE STUDENTS TO GET SICK MORE FREQUENTLY.

Although these useful automatic reactions are meant for survival, the physiological responses to perceived threats and the necessity of reacting to them over time might also create a sense of lethargy and fatigue. Jensen (1998) notes that studies show chronic stress can result in a depressed immune system, which can cause students to get sick more frequently (53). And Sylwester notes that problems arise when students remain in reflexive mode without developing reflective skills that are necessary to solve problems in conscious, deliberate, creative ways. Thus it is important to help students bring their reflective systems online.

Even as we defensively react to stress or threat, we size up the situation and create a plan. The brain shifts from reaction to action. As Joseph LeDoux (1996) explains, "In responding first with its most-likely-to-succeed behavior, the brain buys time . . . Eventually you take control. You make a plan and carry it out. This requires that your cognitive resources be directed to the emotional problem. You have to stop thinking about whatever you were thinking about before the danger occurred and start thinking about the danger you are facing (and already responding to automatically)" (175–76). We quickly review various options and recall previous successes. We predict possible outcomes and prioritize the steps that we want to take. We thoughtfully plan the voluntary action that we want to take to replace the involuntary reaction that saved us initially and bought us some time.

As teachers, we work to reduce the conditions in our environments that induce the reflex response. At the same time, we must help students acquire personal strategies to deal with stress. As Jensen (1998) notes, there are two ways to cope with stress: "One is to manage the conditions that can induce it, and the other is to use personal strategies that mediate and release it. Help students learn about what induces stress and what to do about it" (59). Students can understand what causes them to feel stressed or threatened and learn a variety of ways to cope with and manage that stress. Teaching students about stress and providing practice with patterns of responses will help them learn appropriate actions to take when they are stressed.

The more healthy coping patterns students store, the more possibilities from which they can choose. You can teach a variety of skills and strategies to help students deal with the reflex response:

*time management skills*
*communication skills*
*relationship skills*
*conflict-resolution strategies*
*problem-solving strategies*
*creativity strategies*
*divergent thinking skills*
*anger management*

*relaxation strategies*
*health enhancement and nutrition strategies*
*self-reflection techniques, including keeping a journal*

## Fear and Threat at School

What things at school might students perceive as threat so they respond reflexively, minimizing their capabilities? We know that all students and situations are unique. Some middle and high school students may feel constantly threatened by other students who are gang members. At other campuses, the pressure of grades, awards, competitions, and social standing may cause students to feel stressed. Elementary schools may have bullies, verbally abusive students, and certain kids who dominate others. Even schools with no obvious social problems may have extremely complex schedules and rotations. Many young children may find this kind of atmosphere confusing or even threatening. Students in schools where a variety of languages are spoken in the homes or that have high migrant populations may feel threatened by communication difficulties and possible lack of long-standing relationships. Just being in an environment with hundreds of others may trigger some students to feel threatened.

As a teacher I have witnessed students reacting defensively in the classroom. Test anxiety is a classic example. It is often marked by a physical reflex response: upset stomach, perspiration, dizziness. The brain is actually trying to react to the threat by keeping the students ready. For some students, the reflex response is so overwhelming that it keeps them from performing well on the exam. This reflex response also happens for many students when they are auditioning for a part in the school play, giving an oral report to the class, or even reading aloud.

But besides performances or evaluation situations there are day-to-day events that seem to cause many students to have this reaction. Students may feel threatened by a parent if they don't perform well in school or receive a certain grade. This overwhelming threat may actually cause them to perform worse.

I have seen students become highly emotional or defensive when they are assigned a new book or moved to the next level in a curriculum program. These students respond reflexively to anything new because they perceive a pattern of failure.

Although I have not done a formal study, I can certainly comment on some of my observations. Students' perceptions of whether or not the classroom is a safe and secure environment can influence their reactions. A long-term relationship with a teacher appears to strengthen feelings of safety and reduce anxiety. Other factors seem to relate to personality. Shy, sensitive children often react defensively to some of the most simple assignments and challenges. Students who are risk takers in general react positively to stress or threat.

It is not difficult to generate a list of conditions under which your students are likely to respond reflexively. Although several of the circumstances listed below could challenge or pressure certain students who need that to perform well, in general students are threatened by these events; consider them carefully:

> *fear of potential physical harm from teacher or other students*
>
> *emotional threats, embarrassment, put-downs*
>
> *demonstrated disrespect for self, culture, or social group*
>
> *inadequate time to complete a task*
>
> *lack of time for reflection and expansion*
>
> *predetermined correct outcomes established by an external agent*
>
> *unfamiliar work with little support for learning*
>
> *lack of orderliness and coherence*
>
> *physical and social isolation*
>
> *unknown purpose, schedule, or agenda*
>
> *lack of information about task, behavior expectations, or goals*
>
> *punishments for failure, such as loss of privileges*
>
> *competition and extrinsic rewards*
>
> *perceived irrelevance and lack of personal meaning*

A LONG-TERM RELATIONSHIP WITH A TEACHER APPEARS TO STRENGTHEN FEELINGS OF SAFETY AND REDUCE ANXIETY.

As I noted earlier, using some of these occasionally with some situations may in fact be advantageous, depending on your students and the situation. However, you need to consider every situation carefully. Your relationship with your students will help you make the decision as to when potentially risky techniques might be effective.

## Circle of Influence

Attempting to create a low-threat environment at school doesn't even address the needs of those students who arrive already functioning in survival mode. Most children today are living in stressful environments. The economics of day-to-day living and the lack of emotional familial support are signs of our times. We see more and more children brought to school by siblings, just barely making it in time for the free breakfast program, not knowing where one parent lives and unsure about the other's job or income.

Children from more stable homes may also suffer from prolonged stress and anxiety. Over-scheduled children who have enrichment classes, lessons, or athletic practice almost every day can also feel helpless and fearful. The unreasonable demands on their lives may cause them to react reflexively rather than reflectively.

Fixing what's going on outside of school may be outside your circle of influence, as Jane Healy (1990) would say. Some teachers do get involved with home visits and family support, but that is an unrealistic expectation for most of us. What we must focus on is what we *can* do in our classrooms, in our day-to-day contact with children.

# Creating Schools as Safe Havens

The thought of rethinking *everything* about our school's campus and programs that would contribute to helping kids feel safe sounds overwhelming, impossible even. But creating an environment that is conducive to learning should be our first task, even before implementing the curriculum. It must be the foundation of everything that we do in schools.

Geoffrey and Renate Caine (1997) use the term *relaxed alertness* to describe the tone the school environment should have. It should be a place where harmony exists between the learner's brain and body, anxiety level, and curiosity. The climate must be one of low threat and high challenge. Such creative balance is the challenge for educators.

## Finding Flow

Our first task is to acknowledge the profound effect that stress and threat have on the brain and body. As educators we must first envision, then create environments that provide a low-threat climate. We must also investigate the elements that will maximize capabilities, promote positive behavior, and encourage students to be reflective. Just as we spend time on removing threatening stimuli, we must also consciously provide opportunities for students to experience joy, success, and satisfaction.

Psychologist and author Mihaly Csikszentmihalyi (1990) proposes an easy-to-understand suggestion in *Flow*. For thirty years his team studied states of "optimal experience," that is, times when people report feelings of deep concentration and enjoyment. He uses the term *flow* to describe a state of concentration that is so completely focused it amounts to absolute absorption in an activity. During a flow experience, the mind and body are in complete harmony. Self-consciousness, negative feelings, worries, and anxiety disappear. The activity takes on personal meaning, is intrinsically motivating, and results in total satisfaction.

Athletes reflect such flow when they refer to being in the "zone." Musicians and artists comment on having optimal flow experiences when they are deep in a creative mode or performing. You can apply the flow theory to any situation in which you are having or trying to create a positive enjoyable experience.

A central condition of flow is the balance between the challenge presented and the skills of the person to meet the challenge. If the experience challenges the student beyond what he feels capable of, he might feel anxious and respond reflexively. Conversely, if a student feels her skills are much greater than the task demands,

DURING A FLOW EXPERIENCE, THE MIND AND BODY ARE IN COMPLETE HARMONY. SELF-CONSCIOUSNESS, NEGATIVE FEELINGS, WORRIES, AND ANXIETY DISAPPEAR. THE ACTIVITY TAKES ON PERSONAL MEANING, IS INTRINSICALLY MOTIVATING, AND RESULTS IN TOTAL SATISFACTION.

Csikszentmihalyi notes that there are eight major components of flow:

- ✦ It occurs when we confront tasks we have a chance of completing.

- ✦ We must be able to concentrate on what we are doing.

- ✦ The task has clear goals.

- ✦ The task provides immediate feedback.

- ✦ Deep but effortless involvement removes from our awareness worries and frustrations of everyday life.

- ✦ The experience is an enjoyable one that allows us to exercise a sense of control over our actions.

- ✦ The concern for self disappears.

- ✦ The sense of time is altered; hours pass by in what seems like minutes.

(49)

she may become bored. Students are most likely to experience flow if the challenge is balanced with their self-perceived skills.

## Implications for Educators

Is it possible to create an environment that has an "absence of threat," as Leslie Hart (1998) suggests we shoot for? Given the wide variety of people, there really is no such thing as an absence of threat for everyone. The trick is to create a classroom and school environment in which the majority of students don't feel threatened but do feel greatly challenged. This type of setting allows natural learning to take place. Joyful, rigorous learning should be our first goal. Creating schools that focus on simultaneously engaging the learner's intellect, emotions, creativity, and whole body must be the second goal.

As we begin to understand the overwhelming effects of stress, coercion, and threat on the human brain, we must look at traditional classroom discipline and management systems. The strategy many use to control a student's behavior must not also be the very thing that sets up another defensive reaction. We must shift our thinking to creating systems that promote optimal experiences. By designing instructional strategies and orchestrating systems that are based on flow theory and common sense, we can create truly brain-compatible learning environments.

I have developed the ideas I share here over the last fifteen years as I have explored the brain research and tried to integrate the new understandings into my classroom practices. For veteran teachers, some of the ideas may be updated variations on some tried-and-true techniques, as well as an acknowledgment of the good things you are already doing. For newer teachers, suggestions at the end of each chapter give places to begin. While your intention may be to implement many brain-based strategies and learner-centered approaches eventually, your own brain can handle only so much new information before you yourself begin to have a reflexive response! I recommend using my motto: "I have every intention of doing it all, but I have the common sense to know that I can't do it all at once!"

## *Where to Begin*

I strongly recommend that you familiarize yourself with some of the latest research. Even if you don't read the following books from cover to cover, you should at least have them in your professional library for reference.

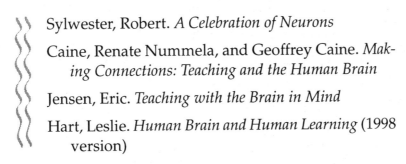

Sylwester, Robert. *A Celebration of Neurons*

Caine, Renate Nummela, and Geoffrey Caine. *Making Connections: Teaching and the Human Brain*

Jensen, Eric. *Teaching with the Brain in Mind*

Hart, Leslie. *Human Brain and Human Learning* (1998 version)

# 2
# Welcome Home

## *Creating an Atmosphere of Relaxed Alertness*

## Begin with the Brain

*The learning environment must be orchestrated in a way that promotes a positive emotional climate as well as providing enriched complex experiences in a physically comfortable space.*

Research has confirmed that a stressful physical environment is linked to student failure, although low to moderate stress is not necessarily detrimental to successful learning. Many studies have confirmed that by paying attention to the physical details in the learning environment (lighting, temperature, color, air quality, seating, design), educators can enhance students' success. Many studies suggest that music may also play a significant role in the learning process. Research indicates that the brain responds to novelty and that there should be changes in the decor every two to four weeks.

# Can We Do It?

First things first. Is it possible to create a classroom and school environment that might actually prevent stress and lessen threat? This kind of classroom would not be a source of confusion for children and would not induce a sense of anxiety or frustration. Wouldn't our time be well spent if we focused our energy on this kind of preventive strategy? Renate and Geoffrey Caine (1994) introduce the idea of creating and maintaining an atmosphere of relaxed alertness: "To maximize learning, we need to establish an environment that allows for safe risk taking. In essence, we need to eliminate pervasive or continuous threat. The sense of safety that welcomes appropriate risks is one part of what we mean by relaxation" (141).

Relaxed alertness is not the same as being calm and mellow. The goal is to create a climate that balances low threat with evidences of challenge for a wide range of students' interests and abilities. The environment must still have tasks, projects, displays, symbols, and clues that will instigate students' intrinsic motivation and attract their interest, attention, and curiosity. If they feel comfortable, then they will not put barriers up and therefore will be open to possibilities of reflection and engagement.

Some educators' concern rises when they hear about relaxed alertness. To a few teachers it may sound like a "warm fuzzy" strategy from the 1970s or 1980s that promoted an open classroom complete with bean-bag chairs, incense, ficus plants, hanging beads in the doorways, strange music on the boom box. While any of these decorations might be appropriate in creating a brain-compatible environment, the key is whether or not the environment and program encourage students and demand that they be alert and fully engaged. When you achieve this balance of comfort, security, and stimulation, you have created an atmosphere of relaxed alertness.

Several years ago I helped restructure Monarch Community School, a very small alternative public elementary. It had been a nonneighborhood school that provided a choice for parents and students. Although the original goals of the school were in line with many brain-based strategies, most students did not feel challenged

RELAXED ALERTNESS IS NOT THE SAME AS BEING CALM AND MELLOW. THE GOAL IS TO CREATE A CLIMATE THAT BALANCES LOW THREAT WITH EVIDENCES OF CHALLENGE FOR A WIDE RANGE OF STUDENTS' INTERESTS AND ABILITIES.

15

at all. The program stated that it was student centered and insisted that students would be motivated to initiate their own learning. My observations were that, while students may have felt free to explore and learn at their own pace, they didn't. Because of the philosophy of the program at the time, teachers rarely introduced new things to students or encouraged them to engage in challenging tasks. This purist view of student-centered learning is missing a key factor in the basic idea of relaxed alertness: high challenge.

In restructuring Monarch School, we strove to achieve a balance between safe and secure, brain-compatible learning environments and high challenges for all of the diverse students. This kind of balanced environment doesn't leave powerful learning to chance. Rather, it regularly orchestrates key experiences for all and can still ensure that students are learning and meeting basic standards.

Later, after the initial restructuring of the school, several students transferred from a local private school modeled after the Sudbury Valley School. The Sudbury School operates on the principle that students should initiate their own activities and learning based solely on their natural curiosity. Those students often reflected that in that totally free environment they may have felt safe, but commented that they were often bored and didn't know what to choose to do. Their comments reflect the ideas expressed in Csikszentmihalyi's flow theory. Without someone to introduce them to challenges and new tasks, they tended to gravitate back to computer games and basic creative play day after day, which eventually led to boredom.

A brain-compatible environment that maintains a climate of relaxed alertness does not leave learning to chance. You don't abandon powerful challenging experiences with the idea that students might be too intimidated or react with a reflex response. Instead, you must begin to form relationships with students to understand each one's challenge threshold, that point where the new task or challenge is too great and the child begins to feel anxious and overwhelmed. If students begin to respond reflexively, we lose valuable learning time.

A BRAIN-COMPATIBLE ENVIRONMENT THAT MAINTAINS A CLIMATE OF RELAXED ALERTNESS DOES NOT LEAVE LEARNING TO CHANCE. YOU DON'T ABANDON POWERFUL CHALLENGING EXPERIENCES WITH THE IDEA THAT STUDENTS MIGHT BE TOO INTIMIDATED OR REACT WITH A REFLEX RESPONSE.

# Multiage and Looping Programs

Understanding each child's challenge threshold is one of the main reasons that I am such an advocate of multiage and looping class-rooms. When teachers have an opportunity to work with students for longer than the traditional nine-month school year, they gain so much greater understanding of each unique student. Teachers will often say that the first month of school is when they get to know their students' abilities, interests, and strengths. In a multiage (two or three grade levels mixed together) or looping classroom (single graded, but teacher moves with entire class up to next grade), students may stay with the same teacher for two or three years.

At Monarch I had students for three years in a multiage fourth-, fifth-, and sixth-grade class. We also had a buddy primary class, that is, a first-, second-, and third-grade class that we worked with regularly. Each year, when the sixth graders moved on, we would welcome the incoming fourth graders. My students and I already knew the incoming fourth graders because they had been in our primary buddy class. By getting to know the students and form-ing a long-term relationship with them, I was able to keep them in the optimal learning flow and maximize their learning. It was not uncommon on the first day of school to see the returning students greet me with a big hug, bring in their materials, find a seat, start copying the daily agenda, and be ready to get started on the first task. Many of them had projects from June in their portfolios, and they got them out and continued working on them!

You can maintain a "welcome home" atmosphere in classrooms that have students that have as much as a four- or five-year differ-ence in age. Arriving in this kind of familial climate in familiar physical settings immediately relieves the stress, anxiety, and con-fusion that many students experience every year as they begin in a new classroom. Familiar faces, things, procedures, and experi-ences keep students ready. Younger students are able to observe older students take on challenges and are therefore more willing to be risk takers themselves. By observing others' success, stu-dents are less intimidated by the challenges and take them on as the logical next step in their learning.

BY GETTING TO KNOW THE STUDENTS AND FORMING A LONG-TERM RELATIONSHIP WITH THEM, I WAS ABLE TO KEEP THEM IN THE OPTI-MAL LEARNING FLOW AND MAXIMIZE THEIR LEARNING.

17

There are many multiage and looping models. The Society for Developmental Education in New Hampshire is an excellent resource for these types of programs. They provide workshops around the country, and they have a wide variety of books for teachers and parents that support the rationale for maintaining a multiage program. Their motto is "Childhood should be a journey, not a race."

# A Teacher's Role

When you arrive at someone's home at the appropriate time, how do you feel if your host or hostess seems disheveled, is incompletely dressed for the occasion, makes excuses, or is still making last-minute preparations? "I guess I shouldn't be here yet." "Maybe I got the time wrong." "She's not ready for me." "Maybe I should wait outside." "I must be inconveniencing her." We feel wonderful, however, when we are greeted at the door by our hostess who is obviously ready and expecting us: ""Hello! I've been anxiously awaiting your arrival! I'm so glad you're here!" Just as the host and hostess create a first impression when they greet and welcome you into their home, so you will create a first impression of the learning environment when you greet your students.

As the host or hostess for your classroom, you should be prepared. *Believe me*, I know how difficult it can be! As a busy parent of my own two children, it is often a challenge to get up and get ready so that I can have that welcoming appearance for my students. It often means spending a little more time during the afternoon to prepare things for class the next day. Of course, there will often be emergencies and extenuating circumstances, but regularly check to see if you are looking like an emergency just happened *every day.* What message does that send to your students? We are the human connection to the learning environment. Our looks, words, attitude, constancy, knowledge, self-respect, and authority will influence how students regard the rest of the room and the tasks at hand.

## Welcome Aboard

It is important to be friendly and encourage students. Be sure to stand near the entrance as they come in. Smile and make eye contact with all students as they enter the room. A handshake or a hand on the shoulder or arm will immediately break the ice and make your first connection. As Harry Wong and Rosemary Tripi Wong (1991) note, "When significant people use significant words and actions, they increase the likelihood of receiving positive behaviors from other people" (77). Wong and Wong also note that the effective teacher does the following:

- ☆ Addresses people by their names and pronounces the names correctly
- ☆ Says "Please" and "Thank you"
- ☆ Has a controlled, disarming smile
- ☆ Is lovable and capable (77)

## Teacher Prestige

Many people refer to a teacher's prestige as a factor in how students perceive her or him. As Renate and Geoffrey Caine (1994) note, "Prestige [in this case] does not refer to popularity, position, power, or fame. It refers to the *authority* that teachers have in the eyes of students by virtue of the sort of people they are and the knowledge they are able to share" (144). Prestige is often communicated by the degree with which teachers' actions and behavior mirror what they say. Incongruence between words and behavior lowers a teacher's prestige in the students' eyes. The trust is damaged due to the lack of honesty and integrity.

The Caines (1994) also note that "Teacher prestige involves the teacher's knowledge of subject matter" (145). Teachers must show their mastery of the topic at hand as well as their interest in discovering more. Your interactions with students must demonstrate your grounding in and grasp of the subject by adding more information as the opportunity comes up, and also your willingness to admit not knowing an answer and expressing interest in finding out.

## Appearance

I can remember having debates with colleagues over appropriate attire for teachers. I am a product of the 1960s and 1970s and began teaching during a fairly progressive era in the very casual area of the central California coast. Jeans and a sweatshirt seemed to work just fine as my teaching uniform. I have since worked at schools that had dress codes for teachers and students, and I have also worked outside of the school system. My best recommendation is that teachers dress appropriately for the area and school in which they teach. If we want our students and the community to treat us with respect, then we should dress as professionals. But my goal is also to dress appropriately for the tasks at hand, which means that on some school days I will wear jeans and a sweatshirt, especially if we are building, gardening, doing other messy projects, designing sets, and so on. But what I wear on the first day of school will send a message that will last the whole year, maybe a lifetime.

Dressing professionally means that you view the job of teaching with the same importance as a job in a bank, a business, or a law firm. It will give you instant credibility that may or may not have come eventually because of your actions. The way you dress will give you some authority and power. On the first day of school, I dress as if I'm going to an interview, because I am being reviewed by students for a job I hope to do with them. You let others know that they are important enough to dress up for. Dressing professionally also shows others that you care about yourself and your appearance, and that it is important to you how others see you.

Whether it be wild jewelry or a wacky tie, a good rule of thumb is to wear nothing that distracts the students. Certainly they might notice and even comment, but if anything about your appearance seems to distract students or be a source of potential ridicule, then it probably is too much.

WHAT I WEAR ON THE FIRST DAY OF SCHOOL WILL SEND A MESSAGE THAT WILL LAST THE WHOLE YEAR, MAYBE A LIFETIME.

## Classroom Environment

Carol Venolia (1988) states, "Disharmonious environments can be sources of physical and mental stress" (10). So any environment in which you are planning on spending time should include the key elements that promote health, relaxation, and positive emotional feelings. The environment should encourage interaction, be aesthetically pleasing, and above all else, do no physical harm.

If our goal is to promote student learning by maintaining an atmosphere of relaxed alertness, then we must evaluate the physical environment to see what elements might cause students to feel stressed, threatened, confused, or anxious. By doing so we can actually circumvent potential problems and work on prevention. Many refer to such evaluation of the environment as "front-end alignment" as we set the stage for powerful, successful learning.

Whether you are trying to improve an existing classroom or design a new learning environment, there are a variety of things to keep in mind. In architect Carol Venolia's (1988) *Healing Environments*, she suggests some qualities we should strive to employ to improve the healthfulness of a place.

> *stimulation of positive awareness of ourselves [and our students!]*
>
> *enhancement of our connections with nature, culture, and people*
>
> *allowance for privacy*
>
> *lack of possibility for physical harm*
>
> *meaningful, varying stimuli*
>
> *encouragement of times to relax*
>
> *balance of constancy and flexibility*
>
> *beauty (11)*

I've taken these basic qualities, restated them in some cases, combined a few, then looked at ways a teacher may interpret these elements to design a brain-friendly learning environment.

## Build Positive Awareness of Ourselves and Our Students

You can set up the classroom to reflect who you are and to reflect the qualities you like or want to encourage in yourself and your students. Include art you like and pictures of your own family, as well as any projects you are proud of that reflect a piece of you. As a reflection of who your students are, it makes sense to include pieces of students' lives, including class work, projects, art, and others. Include pictures and other artifacts of students' lives, families, and interests outside of school. Also include evidence of their hopes, dreams, and potential. The goal is not necessarily to display it for others, but to display it as a reflection of the students themselves. What you shouldn't do is decorate the room for others: parents, teachers, observers, the principal. Ask yourself, "What message does this environment send to my students?" The classroom should build students' positive awareness of themselves, what makes them happy and gives them hope.

Following are descriptions of ideas I have used successfully in my classrooms. While they focus primarily on students, remember that your classroom must also reflect you. Feel free to take part in the activities and displays yourself. Doing so shows your students that you value yourself as well as them, and that you don't regard the activities you ask them to take part in as beneath you.

### Displaying Students' Work

What is the most brain-compatible way to display students' individual work without the possibility of embarrassing, frustrating, or humiliating them? The obvious answer is to allow individual students to choose when and what they display. Public recognition of their efforts is something that some students have difficulty with and that others thrive on. Avoid a bulletin board or other area with a title like "Our Best Work" that has one of each student's recent spelling tests or all papers that got an *A*. Instead, call such an area "Our Personal Best." Each student selects something from the last week to put up for others to see and perhaps acknowledge. Occasionally, students might have nothing they care to share. It just wasn't a great week or they are working on a long-term project or product. Allow such students to pass on having their work displayed.

You could also allow students to create team bulletin boards. I have assigned a display area in the room to each table team. They are responsible for creating the display and presenting information. They have a certain time each week to meet and decide what will go up. They must include at least some of their work. Sometimes they display only their team members' stuff. Other times, they organize and take one topic or product. For instance, Team B may decide to display the water quality graphs that we did in mixed teams. Team D may display the most recent limericks some students wanted to share. A necessary goal is to represent every student somewhere on the boards.

Place comment sheets next to the areas so that other students might write down positive thoughts and feelings about the work. You must first establish a degree of respect and trust among students for this to be successful. You must also ensure that students understand they are to write only positive comments.

### *Personal Posters*

Allow students to create and display personal posters. You might have everyone participate at the beginning of the year, or assign one week to each student as a variation of the "Student of the Week" activity. Each student brings a few pictures from home—photographs of them when they were little, of family members, of pets, and of them doing things they like. They attach the photographs to a medium-sized poster with magazine cut-outs of favorite stars, cars, toys, foods, and so on. As a variation, you might

GOOD IDEA

have a table team do their posters the same week and display them in their assigned classroom area.

You might choose to make the posters into graffiti boards. I provide small self-stick notes, and students write positive comments and compliments about the student and put them right on the poster. Again, you must establish a sense of mutual respect, trust, and guidelines first.

You could also make the poster assignment one of self-portraits and collages of favorites. Instead of photographs, students simply create a collage of all their favorite subjects in school, hobbies, sports, and other pastimes.

### "Mirror, Mirror, on the Wall . . ."

Don't forget the obvious! What better item to have in a classroom that "reflects" positive self-awareness than a mirror. I've had large mirrors hung low enough for small children to see their whole bodies. In secondary school, I had a secret cabinet that had a 12-by-18-inch mirror inside the door. This secret mirror was so popular with everyone that I often had students who weren't even in my class stopping by between classes to sneak a peak and check hair, lipstick, clothes, and so on.

### Real Things from Home

Students love to bring in personal items to share or just to have with them at school. Of course, sometimes it's necessary to make specific rules about the items. In self-contained classrooms, I often let students have an area of their desks or tables that they can use for displaying something special. Yes, I even let them tape pictures and things right onto the surface. It will be their responsibility later to remove them and clean the area. If your students have cubbies, consider allowing them to decorate the cubbies or have little creatures or action figures that live in there. Students bring in baseball cards, pictures of rock stars, stickers, skateboard decals, even little Koosh creatures. Make sure you have clear guidelines to ensure that others don't mess with the items.

Don't forget that even high school kids like personal items with them. In secondary classrooms, I kept a basket for each team. I labeled the baskets according to the period and team, for example, "Period 1: Green Team" or "Table B, Third Period." Students keep Beanie Babies, stress balls, cute erasers, and so on in the baskets. They put the baskets on a shelf when their class time is over.

### Your Stuff

Make sure that you have an area that reflects you and your interests. It can be a source of inspiration in the middle of a busy day. I always had photographs of my husband, kids, dog, and a picture of me at the age of the students in the class. I had little mementos that kids had given me. Several years ago they started giving me things with apples on them or in the shape of apples. I would display this collection on a shelf near my desk. If you collect certain things, such as butterflies, display some at school. One junior high teacher had a collection of *ugly* neckties. He hung them up on hooks under the chalkboard. He actually used them as hall passes for students when they had to leave during class time. They had to choose one and wear it as they walked in the halls.

## Enhancement of Our Connections and Interactions with Nature, Cultures, and People

Just one hundred years ago humans spent a large percentage of their waking hours outside. Even homemakers spent many hours outside doing laundry, gathering eggs, sowing seeds, making soap, traveling to town. Most of our lives are now dominated by indoor tasks and activities. Even when we go someplace, we simply pass through the outdoors on our way from a building to our cars!

HOW CAN WE EXPECT CHILDREN TO ENGAGE IN LESSONS AND CARE ABOUT ECOLOGY AND CONSERVATION IF THEY HAVEN'T SPENT ENOUGH TIME OUT-DOORS TO APPRECI-ATE IT?

Children spend *much* more time inside than children of previous generations ever did. They simply aren't used to playing outside and exploring the environment. My neighborhood pals and I dug holes, built forts, picked berries, made street coasters, dammed up gutters, ate honeysuckle flowers, and watched clouds. Watching TV all afternoon was simply unacceptable! As a parent I know how hard it is these days to encourage extended outside play, especially during hot or inclement weather when there are so many terrific diversions available inside.

As a result of our indoor society, we have a generation of children who are growing up without a solid understanding of what is just outside the front door. How can we expect children to engage in lessons and care about ecology and conservation if they haven't spent enough time outdoors to appreciate it? Likewise, if they haven't had a chance to connect and interact with other people and cultures in their own neighborhoods and cities, then they have missed a huge opportunity to learn about their peers and classmates. For many their basic understanding of other cultures comes from the media exposure they get, and there is a good chance that this exposure is biased and stereotypical.

You have the opportunity to create a microcosm of the student's real world. Collect items from nature and cultures in your community and school; display them in the classroom. Far better for children to see a basket of various seashells they can touch, smell, and feel than to never have a chance to see them at all! The following suggestions should provide some ideas for ways you can enhance such connections.

## Plants

One easy way to create an enriched natural environment is to bring in a variety of plants. Several varieties are hardy enough to live under the fluorescent lights and chalk dust found in many classrooms: coleus, spider plants, ficus, and of course, many succulents and cacti. Hanging plants near windows can be a beautiful addition to a classroom. Or who can resist the sight of a bouquet of fresh-cut flowers? About once a month I would stop by the farmer's market and pick up a bunch of colorful flowers and greenery. I tried to find the blooms that best represented the season. I encourage you to keep several inexpensive vases in various sizes in your classroom. As students see that you value the beauty of plants and flowers, they will start bringing you some from home or small gift bouquets.

I know several teachers who opt for artificial plants in their rooms, especially if the plants are up high and far away from scrutiny or if they are in an area that simply can't support a live plant. But it always concerns me when teachers tell me that they can't get plants to stay alive in a classroom because the air is too dry or there's not enough sunlight. If plants can't stay alive in an environment, how can we expect children to thrive there?

## Nature Brought Indoors

Designate an area of the classroom as a nature nook. You could use a table, a shelf, or a basket in which you and your students display artifacts from nature for investigation. Rotate the items regularly and encourage students to bring in things. Although this suggestion seems obviously appropriate for elementary classrooms, do not underestimate the power of it in secondary classrooms. Once in a while the items will be things that will be ruined if touched: fragile butterfly wings, thorny thistles, or delicate spider webs. You can display those under glass or in some other way to keep them presentable. However, most of the items in the display should be *do touch* items, such as the following:

*seashells*
*birds' nests*
*driftwood*
*leaves*
*rocks*
*feathers*
*honeycomb*
*unusual vegetables*
*tree bark*
*sand and dirt*
*leather and fur*
*woven baskets*
*bamboo*
*various nuts*

### Fresh Flowers

Find a good source or a parent who could help by bringing in fresh-cut flowers every Monday. During the winter dried arrangements with different ribbons or decorations can reflect the seasons, as well. Set the vase on a place mat in a prominent place for all to enjoy.

### Classroom Animals

Whether it be a kindergarten classroom or a high school English class, I strongly recommend that you consider having real animals in the room. Students should be directly responsible for the upkeep of the pets and also be responsible for taking them home to care for them over vacations. Small furry creatures such as guinea pigs, rats, gerbils, and bunnies seem to be a great choice for younger children. Hamsters are cute, but they tend to sleep all day. In intermediate classrooms, I often kept reptiles and amphibians such as snakes, lizards, iguanas, chameleons, geckos, frogs, and toads that students could handle. Insects such as crickets, praying mantises, and walking sticks are interesting to observe. Tarantulas are another high interest pet. In secondary classrooms where as many as 125 students would pass through the classroom within the course of a day, I usually kept an aquarium with very hardy fish: goldfish, guppies, mollies, catfish.

If your school discourages having classroom pets, consider having pets visit for short periods. Often a child might have a pet that could come and visit for a day or a week. I have seen a few teachers organize a pet pool in which a small pet rotates to each classroom for one week at a time.

Occasionally I have had extreme situations where a student had severe allergies and we couldn't have any living pets in the room. If it's not possible at all, perhaps you can get an idea from a veteran teacher I taught with years ago. On the back counter he had a small cage, complete with sawdust and wood chips in the bottom. In the cage was a stuffed guinea pig. The students rotated the duties of pet monitor. When it was their turn, they could get the pet out of the cage and play with him, exercise him, or just cuddle. They also put little toys in the cage so he wouldn't get bored. It really was quite a joke, but these fourth graders seemed to love the stuffed pet and the teacher, and they still got the idea of what caring for a pet was like.

## *Sounds from Nature*

Although we must be aware of how much noise and miscellaneous sounds our bodies are enduring, we can add some sounds that may soothe and heal. A pleasant wind chime outside a window can add a comforting sound while making us aware of what is going on with the air outside. Quiet bird chirps can be relaxing and can come from a pet or a birdhouse or tree outside a window. Pet crickets chirping and frogs croaking can bring nature into the classroom.

Water is also a very soothing sound. I have visited many classrooms that have a small counter-sized fountain. You can purchase

one at a department store or garden supply shop. I have also seen instructions for making a small gurgling fountain at landscaping supply stores and in magazines. Adjust the pump speed and arrangement of the rocks so that the sound is soothing and babbling. At first, it is not uncommon for students and the teacher alike to comment that the new water sounds increase their need to use the restrooms.

Many audiocassettes and CDs have terrific environmental sounds. Gentle showers that turn into severe thunderstorms may not be as soothing as the steady sound of waves on a beach, so choose carefully. Forest sounds and evening crickets can actually make for a calming buffer against some of the everyday noises that we must endure from things such as lights, fans, heaters, computers.

### Expand the Learning Environment

WE SHOULD BEGIN TO SEE THE LEARNING ENVIRONMENT AS GOING BEYOND THE FOUR WALLS OF THE CLASSROOM.

We should also begin to see the learning environment as going beyond the four walls of the classroom. Is there at least some other space that you might develop at your school? A garden box or LifeLab gardening area is a wonderful place for each classroom to have a little patch of earth to try to grow something. You can investigate creatures, dirt, and the effects of the weather. You can observe seasonal changes over time. Children who say they "hate" vegetables gobble up carrots, peas, celery, and broccoli when they grow and harvest the same vegetables with their own hands.

Some teachers have created small gardens in half-barrels and put them on wheels (available at garden supply stores). The minigardens can be wheeled inside at night if the weather is too harsh or security is an issue. Some classrooms have adopted a tree or planter box that already exists on the campus. They post a sign that indicates that the area has been "Adopted by Room 4" and take responsibility for watering, cleaning, weeding, and so on.

Some teachers have facilitated students' efforts to adopt an area near the school to clean and protect. A local creek bed, park, fountain, and highway offer terrific opportunities for students to become responsible stewards. A key is to keep up the efforts for a whole year so that students can see the results of their efforts and to see what changes happen over time. You can study the cleanliness of an area, the growth, and the impact that humans have on your chosen place.

### Bringing in People

Just as we expand our learning environment to include outside places, so we should consider expanding our exposure to other people in the community. Career days are a great way to introduce kids to the multitude of opportunities awaiting them.

You can also make regular visits to a local nursing home, a public library, a senior center, a preschool, a corner store, a hospital, other businesses. Such field trips give children rich experiences with real people beyond the four walls of a classroom.

### Celebrate Cultural Diversity

Every community of learners has a rich cultural background that should be showcased often through classroom projects and presentations. If there are celebrations or holidays observed in the community, consider allowing students, families, and other community members to share traditions and customs with the class. But I pass on a word of caution I received from Ventura Lopez-Cardona, a dynamic California administrator I had the pleasure of knowing. He encouraged teachers to be careful of trivializing cultures by celebrating only holidays. When we honor a culture only through its holidays, we tend to stereotype the people, traditions, and the celebration itself. Celebrating the influence of the Chinese in our community should go beyond learning about the Chinese New Year. Likewise, leprechauns and shamrocks don't really teach me anything about my Irish heritage.

WHEN WE HONOR A CULTURE ONLY THROUGH ITS HOLIDAYS, WE TEND TO STEREOTYPE THE PEOPLE, TRADITIONS, AND THE CELEBRATION ITSELF.

Look for opportunities throughout the year for families to bring in heirlooms, pictures, and other artifacts. Share favorite family recipes, music, and games. Displaying evidence in the classrooms of the rich cultural heritage of our communities will help build an awareness of and respect for ourselves and our community.

## Private Places and Spaces

A classroom with anywhere from fifteen to thirty-five students is one of the most difficult places to provide private spaces and places. Yet we know that humans have their need for control over the environment and crave at least some place that they can call their own, where they can be masters or mistresses of their domains. Adolescents also begin to feel territorial and seem to stake out areas of their own. In a middle school classroom some dominant students may actually seem to mark their territory using what we may consider to be crude methods.

HAVING AT LEAST A SEMIPRIVATE PLACE FOR STUDENTS TO GO FOR SHORT PERIODS OF TIME CAN GIVE THEM A CHANCE TO REFLECT, CALM THEMSELVES, AND REGROUP TO BUILD THE ENERGY IT TAKES TO INTERACT WITH OTHERS.

Having at least a semiprivate place for students to go for short periods of time can give them a chance to reflect, calm themselves, and regroup to build the energy it takes to interact with others. And according to Howard Gardner's multiple intelligence theory, students strong in the intrapersonal intelligence will have a strong need to think, process, and problem solve in such privacy. It is imperative that we provide these students with a quiet, protected area and the time in which to process information and experiences.

Other students will use private places more as places for their things. In a traditional self-contained classroom with desks, students have a private place for their things that has some sense of security. For students who sit at tables or who are required to move among different work areas or classrooms, it will be important to provide places that are their personal space.

### *Cubbies and Bins*

In classrooms that have team tables or other group seating, it is important to provide baskets, bins, or cubbies for students to keep their private things and works in progress. Cubbies should be at least large enough to fit a three ring notebook, books, and a pencil box. I recommend that you provide plastic bins that can be pulled out of the cubbies like drawers to afford more privacy. These bins also keep little things from falling or rolling out. Students can also take the bins to their desks or work areas, then return them to the cubbies when they are through.

### Portable Baskets or Packs

If cubbies aren't possible or practical, there are other ways to provide private, secure places for students' things. Some classrooms have plastic or cardboard book baskets that belong to the individual children and have their names on them. Students can set the baskets on top of their tables and transport them easily to other work areas. One year my students made cloth packs that fit over the backs of their chairs. These were less bulky than regular backpacks, but still had a flap over the top to provide a private space for their books and other materials.

### Reflection or Take Five Zone

Create a small space within the classroom that can be a place for reflecting. This corner area could have a comfortable chair or couch as well as soothing and quiet items. Set standards and time limits: everyone has a right to go to the Take Five Zone for up to five minutes with no questions asked. If, after five minutes, individual students are still there, then perhaps they want you to ask why they are there. For an introverted student, an intrapersonal thinker, or a student who is simply having a rough day, this kind of refuge can make a difference in attitude and overall school experience.

GOOD IDEA

GOOD IDEA

Following is a list of items you could have in the take five zone:

> *rocking chair*
> *fish tank*
> *lava lamp*
> *tape player*
> *books and magazines*
> *lamp*
> *stuffed animals*
> *photo albums*
> *journals*

Of course, there is the chance that many students will flock to the corner at first, but I assure you that once the novelty has worn off, students will use the zone for its designed purpose. You will soon see that some students stop there frequently and others rarely go there.

### *Forts and Hidey Places*

There's nothing more inviting to students than a small hidey place that only a few of them can fit into at a time. Kids used to have more opportunities to build forts and tree houses in their own backyards. Many of today's children don't have an outside or inside place that they can go to for secret meetings or private, quiet times.

In your classroom, you can place a small cushion under a table. I once saw a classroom whose teacher had converted an old coatroom into a book nook. In primary classrooms sometimes playhouses and puppet theaters can serve this purpose. Of course, as with any of these ideas, you need to establish appropriate times and procedures with your students.

## Sense of Security from Physical Harm

There are many kinds of physical harm, and perhaps the first called to mind is that caused by other people. However, I deal with that elsewhere through guidelines, procedures, and other strategies. In this section, I focus only on environmental safety.

Carol Venolia (1988) writes, "It seems obvious that we would not want to make buildings that harm our bodies—yet it's being done every day. Toxic materials, stressful lighting, unnerving noise, and unhealthy heating and air conditioning systems can all work against our well-being and are present, to varying degrees, in many contemporary buildings" (64). Schools across America have already had to address problems such as asbestos in the walls, formaldehyde under the flooring, and a variety of toxic chemicals used routinely in science and art classrooms. Research suggests that factors in addition to chemicals in today's classrooms may also do us physical harm, and that we are only just beginning to understand the effects on us and our students. Yet we do know that there is a connection between physical health and the ability of the brain to function at effective levels. To create truly brain-compatible classrooms, we must include body-compatible environments.

*The Healthy School Book* edited by Norma L. Miller (1995) is an excellent resource for those interested in addressing environmental issues that may be affecting their students' health. The book cites comprehensive research done at Texas Women's University that established ten areas of major concern regarding maintaining ecological guidelines that ensure a healthy learning environment. They are listed here in order of their importance:

1. heating, cooling and ventilation, with proper maintenance being a top priority
2. improper use of and overexposure to pesticides
3. cleaning products that produce toxic fumes and irritate skin
4. chemicals ranging from those used in copy machines to those in art and science labs
5. fragrances such as perfumes and air fresheners
6. sites near major highways, railroads, airports, television or radio stations, microwave towers, high-power electric lines, toxic dumps, or garbage incinerators
7. lack of natural or full-spectrum lighting and inadequate lighting in classrooms
8. installation of new floors, painting, roof repairs, and other remodeling

TOXIC MATERIALS, STRESSFUL LIGHTING, UNNERVING NOISE, AND UNHEALTHY HEATING AND AIR CONDITIONING SYSTEMS CAN ALL WORK AGAINST OUR WELL-BEING AND ARE PRESENT, TO VARYING DEGREES, IN MANY CONTEMPORARY BUILDINGS.
—CAROL VENOLIA

35

9. floors that contain toxic substances and carpets that are not steam cleaned at least two times a year to remove allergens, dirt, and dust mites

10. toxic art supplies or those not designed specifically for children; nontoxic art products are labeled "conforms to ASTM-D4236"

All these areas and more deserve our attention. Several studies on the effects of lighting in a classroom conclude that students' vision, fatigue levels, attendance, posture, and infection rate were negatively affected by the standard lighting found in classrooms. Schools located near agricultural areas also must contend with toxic pesticides and fertilizers that are applied to crops. So many illnesses in children these days may be caused by the closed air systems that many schools have. Our responsibility as educators is to keep ourselves and our students healthy, watch for negligent practices, and be vigilant about creating healthful learning environments. Depending on the severity of the unhealthiness of the environment, you may want to begin to take stronger action. Seek support from other teachers, parents, and your principal. Begin to discover what would solve the problem.

> OUR RESPONSIBILITY AS EDUCATORS IS TO KEEP OURSELVES AND OUR STUDENTS HEALTHY, WATCH FOR NEGLIGENT PRACTICES, AND BE VIGILANT ABOUT CREATING HEALTHFUL LEARNING ENVIRONMENTS.

## Meaningful, Varying Stimuli

Sometimes I will visit a classroom and there are so many decorations or student projects hanging from the walls and ceilings that I can hardly see the students! When our senses are overstimulated and we are bombarded with input, we may shut down in self-defense. But we can also get frustrated and bored with the monotony of a sterile environment. As Venolia (1988) states, "When we are exposed to unchanging temperature, lighting levels, noise, and sights, and when nothing around us moves or grows, our senses become dull and we function poorly" (13).

### *Thematic Realia and Artifacts*

Include around the learning environment, including the classroom and the hallways, a variety of hands-on, *do-touch* materials related to what the students are studying. Encourage students to bring in books, tapes, stuffed toys, and other items connected to the study theme. If the curriculum is relevant, you will be amazed at how much they start bringing in.

### *Interactive, Engaging Stimuli*

Bring in interesting puzzles, games, art supplies, and other items that will help students develop their skills. Provide stimuli that address a wide range of developmental abilities. You will be surprised at how older children will be attracted to some rather primary toys or games. These items don't necessarily have to relate to your current unit of study; they are important just for giving students a break or keeping them interested.

### *Choice Centers*

Centers are a perfect place to bring in a variety of activities that students can rotate to use. Select materials that you can display for one-week periods. Students who are attracted to those particular activities will keep coming back and looking forward to the next time those items are in the center.

37

## Encouragement of Times to Relax

If you can, provide physical spaces that promote relaxation such as the take five zone mentioned earlier. You can also orchestrate certain times of the day or class time in which to encourage students to rest, relax, and experience calm.

As I note in chapter 5, students also need opportunities to have fun! Do you plan playful times? Can you let yourself and your students get silly without feeling like you are losing control or respect? Parties and celebrations certainly help. Consider doing something playful daily.

### *Quiet Times*

You can often most easily help students relax by simply designating a time for silent reading, or "Drop Everything and Relax" (DEAR). Students love it if during this quiet relaxing time they can sit on the floor or wherever they want. Although I originally set this time aside for reading, you may allow some students to do something else quietly, if they like; otherwise they'll feel stressed instead of relaxed.

### *Couches and Cushions*

There is nothing more homey and secure than a comfy small couch, cushion, or beanbag chair. However, I'm pretty picky about the quality of the items I have in the classroom. Cleanliness is imperative, and items with visible stuffing or springs are not acceptable. Occasionally because of head lice or other health issues, you will have to avoid having any furniture with natural cloth coverings. Although not as comfortable, you can find decent beanbag chairs and futon cushions in vinyl fabrics that clean up easily. I have often had parents donate high-quality items. Futon-type mattresses or chairs are also great for a classroom. You need to establish appropriate procedures for using the items.

In such private places, you'll often find students in almost fetal positions as they read or rest. It is also a joy to see a couple of students leaning against each other sharing some quiet time. In secondary classrooms, having a couch in your room will attract students from everywhere.

### A Joke a Day

Assign students different days to share jokes with the class. This assignment opens up great discussions about boundaries, appropriateness, and respect. You should really screen younger children's jokes.

### Anti-Coloring Books and MadLibs

An excellent commercial product with which students have fun is Susan Striker's Anti-Coloring Book series. The coloring books have simple, one-page activities that encourage creative thinking, inventiveness, and playfulness. MadLibs are also a great tool for engaging the whole class in a game that teaches parts of speech, with a comical reading at the end of a session.

## Balance of Constancy and Flexibility

Our brains and bodies will most likely feel uncomfortable if there is too much externally imposed rigidity or constant confusion and change. We must work to achieve a balance between things that students can count on to stay the same and elements that students can count on to change regularly.

WARM LIGHTING, CURTAINS ON WINDOWS, A WELCOME MAT, SOOTHING MUSIC, AND A REFRESHING SCENT MIGHT BE COMFORTING SIGNS STUDENTS CAN COUNT ON.

When students arrive in the classroom there should be a variety of things they can count on: daily agendas, weekly and monthly calendars, attendance and lunch management systems, procedures for exchanging assignments and homework, where to go for missed work. They will also begin to count on the ambience of a room. A particular design theme or color scheme could be your signature in a room. Warm lighting, curtains on windows, a welcome mat, soothing music, and a refreshing scent might be comforting signs students can count on.

At the end of one year a fifth-grade boy told me he always liked coming in and smelling my perfume. I thanked him, but I told him I didn't think it was me. I had him investigate the room to see if he could find the source of the pleasant, subtle scent he described. He eventually found a lamp ring on a lamp on a back table. He commented that all year he had loved the peachy smell in our room and had just always assumed it had been me.

It is also refreshing to enter a room and see changes from time to time. Decorations that reflect seasonal changes or thematic changes in the curriculum can be motivational and engage curiosity (see chapter 6). A thoughtful change in the arrangement of the furniture or areas of the room can also give students a feeling of a fresh start or a new beginning.

### Theme Corner

Have one area designated as a display area for the class's current theme unit, novel study, service project, or current events. While students may want the rest of the class to be constant, they will appreciate the frequent changes that might go on in this area.

### Shifting Perspective

Occasionally, when I have needed to have a fresh start or to shake things up a bit, I have totally inverted the classroom perspective by turning the front of a classroom into the back. Sometimes I moved my desk or a screen and overhead projector. It certainly helped get classes out of a rut. Involve students in proposing possible changes.

## Beauty

As Venolia (1988) says, "The creation and experience of beauty is immediate, whole, and healing. It enlivens our senses, warms our hearts, relaxes us, and puts us at one with the entire surround" (15). Even small touches of beauty enhance subliminal learning and feelings of well-being. Take time to bring beauty into the learning environment. Check out posters and art prints from school resource collections and public libraries to display in an area. Students will notice and admire objets d'art such as small statues, wall hangings, pottery, and sculpture, and will appreciate your thoughtful additions to the classroom.

## *Where to Begin*

Of the many ideas suggested in this chapter, there are two I believe you should attend to no matter what!

1. Work hard to make a *great* first impression. Greet the students personally on the first day. If at all possible, be at the door every morning with a smile. This kind of positive connection will begin to build a personal relationship with your students that they will not forget.

2. Select a classroom environment suggestion you can implement easily. Write a letter to parents that asks for contributions. Your wish list can be broad or narrow. I send one of these wish lists home at the beginning of the year and mid-year. I am always amazed at the responses I get from families. Even parents who are struggling financially often send in a few items. On page 42 is a sample letter that could go home to parents.

# Back to School

Dear Families:

As your children's teacher this year, I will be trying hard to capture their attention, challenge them, and motivate them to be life-long learners. In my own research I have discovered how important it is to create a pleasant and healthy learning environment. To make our classroom a comfortable place to learn, I am looking for some common items that you may be able to donate. If you can contribute or lend any of the following items, please call me at the number listed below. Thanks for supporting your children's school!

healthy potted plants
wall hooks to hang plants
vases
small area rugs
welcome mat
table lamps
fish tank with pump
lava lamp (do you still have one?)
small baskets for materials
sheer, cafe curtains and rods
place mats (6 matching)
large coffee mugs (for pencils)
prints of art
framed art
small statues or sculpture
sun catcher (hangs in window)
suction hooks (for glass)
a framed wall mirror
a small candy bowl or jar
seasonal flags or banners
small wall clock
extension cord

Sincerely,

Martha Kaufeldt

# 3
# Patterns and Procedures

*Organizing Systems for Orderliness*

## Begin with the Brain

*The brain innately seeks to detect familiar and useful patterns in its environment. These patterns give a context to what otherwise might be interpreted as meaningless. These meaningful patterns, when practiced, become wired in the brain as programs.*

The brain seeks to make order out of chaos. It organizes and associates new information according to previous experiences or similar circumstances. You can establish patterns of appropriate behavior and systems for doing things in a classroom. These logical patterns create an organizational strategy for dealing with each type of event or experience that comes up in a classroom. Confusion and frustration will be reduced as the brain feels secure in knowing and detecting the pattern for appropriate behavior.

# Classroom Systems

When students arrive in your classroom, they will notice you first, get the feel of the environment second, then begin to scan the room for clues as to how the place runs. Older students may be looking for classmates and peers whom they know. Younger children are interested in what centers, displays, and toys are out. And *everyone* wants to know where she will sit!

How the systems within the classroom are set up will reflect your basic beliefs about children's behavior. Alfie Kohn (1996) asks teachers to consider their own assumptions about the motivation behind what children do. Reflect on the following statements. They are often at the heart of more traditional classroom management systems.

☆ Do you think kids are always trying to get away with something?

☆ Do you believe that children should be told exactly what to do and what will happen to them if they don't do what they are told?

☆ Do you believe that you should give positive reinforcement to children who do something good or nice if you want them to keep acting that way?

☆ Do you feel that children need to be taught self-restraint, to control their impulses?

☆ Do you believe that children are driven by wanting power, control, or superiority?

☆ Do you believe that children need to feel pain or loss before they will stop behaving badly?

☆ Do you feel that you can identify "troublemakers" early on?

☆ Do you believe that if you give kids an inch, they'll take a mile?

☆ Do you assume that teachers must get and maintain control of the classroom; otherwise there will be chaos?

☆ Do you believe that children are basically untrustworthy, selfish, or aggressive?

WE MUST BEGIN TO CONSIDER WHAT THINGS WE NEED TO PUT IN PLACE FOR CHILDREN TO FLOURISH INSTEAD OF CONSIDERING HOW WE CAN MAKE THEM DO WHAT WE WANT.

When we look at results of brain research, developmental stages of children, and the new information regarding emotions and how we process them (Goleman, LeDoux, Pert), then our views about children, their capabilities, and their needs begin to shift. As Kohn (1996) notes, "Teachers who assume that children are capable of acting virtuously can likewise set into motion a self-fulfilling prophecy . . . We might proceed from the premise that humans are as capable of generosity and empathy as they are of looking out for Number One, as inclined (all things being equal) to help as to hurt" (7–8). As educators develop a more positive view of children and their motivation, the real-world impact will be powerful. We must begin to consider what things we need to put in place for children to flourish instead of considering how we can make them do what we want.

## Classroom Standards and Courtesies

Positively framed prevention strategies are the key here. By establishing, teaching, and rehearsing expected standards and procedures, teachers provide knowledge and experience with examples of the appropriate responses and behaviors for situations students create and encounter in the classroom. First and foremost, you should create a brief list of your basic standards and expectations. The list is not one of rules because they are stated positively. You don't post consequences by the list; students understand that everyone in the classroom will always attempt to meet these basic standards of behavior.

Many classrooms keep their standards simple: "Demonstrate Respect and Responsibility to Yourself, Others, and the Environment." When you think about it, that simple statement really covers everything!

In 1986, Robert Ellingsen, an exceptional classroom teacher, a friend, and at that time a fellow associate of Susan Kovalik, put together what he referred to as "Rules to Live By." He felt strongly that classroom standards should reflect ways responsible adults are expected to behave in the real world. Consequently, he included no "Do Not Do" rules or trivial things; that is, he had no rules such as "Do not chew gum"; "Use only white paper for written assignments." Based somewhat on the *Tribes* (Gibbs 1995) standards (see chapter 4), Ellingsen's "Rules to Live By" proved very effective at a variety of grade levels and were ultimately refined and incorporated into Susan Kovalik's integrated thematic instruction model as "Lifelong Guidelines." Later, Robert and I taught together for four years at Monarch Community School, and the classroom standards evolved into the following.

## Monarch Community School
## Classroom Standards and Expectations

*Be* trustworthy *and* truthful *to others at all times.*

*Be* active listeners; *use your ears, eyes, and heart.*

*Show respect to others by* giving up put-downs.

*Show respect to yourself by always* doing your personal best.

So why a list of standards instead of rules? A classroom rules list does not prevent misbehavior; in fact, rules seem to invite it! Rules were meant to be broken! In Robert DiGiulio's (1995) *Positive Classroom Management,* he states that rules and laws may be necessary in huge societies but inappropriate in the small, more personalized world of a classroom. By associating punishments with broken rules, we teach students that they can trade misbehavior for a short, meaningless time out or other such consequence. Such a system sets up the escalating endless spiral. As DiGiulio notes, "The only thing the teacher can do in response is to raise the stakes by making the punishment increasingly distasteful in the hope that fewer will opt for it" (16).

RULES CAN TRANSFORM ANY CLEVER STUDENT INTO A 'CLASSROOM LAWYER'.
—ROBERT DiGIULIO

DiGiulio goes on to point out that "rules can transform any clever student into a 'classroom lawyer,' engaging the teacher in arguments over the meaning of classroom or school rules" (26–29). He offers a list similar to Ellingsen's classroom standards called "Four Basic Understandings."

47

## Basic Understandings
## That Encourage Prosocial Behavior

1. Respect Is Nonnegotiable
2. Cooperation over Competition
3. Achievement Is Valued
4. Full Inclusion Is Practiced

YOU MUST TEACH COURTESIES CONCRETELY, BY MODELING THEM AND PRACTICING THEM WITHIN THE CLASSROOM.

After establishing standards of behavior, we must discuss with our students what "common courtesy" means. Students of any age can participate in such a discussion. With the discussion comes understanding of the premise that we must honor and respect others until they demonstrate that they are not worthy of our respect. We know students have varied experiences. Many children have not had respectful or courteous role models; they may not even have had opportunities to observe such behavior. In general, you and your students may list some of the following courtesies:

## In General We Can
## Describe Courtesies as

Words and actions that regard and treat other people humanely.

Signs and indication of consideration for others.

Words that communicate feelings of remorse when we make a mistake.

You must teach courtesies concretely, by modeling them and practicing them within the classroom. Such a theme makes for terrific role-play opportunities as students generate possible scenarios.

### *Ms. Manners and Eddie Haskell*

Role-play social situations that give your students practice with courteous language. First brainstorm courteous words and phrases on the board. Then write down several social situations in which someone would have to be courteous: getting in line or getting on a bus, asking someone for an empty chair, accidentally bumping into someone at a store, accidentally spilling something on a stranger. Choose one of the situations at random and ask students to draw it. Then pair them off to act out the scene and insert as many of the courteous phrases as possible. We call this "Eddie Haskell" because students would try to be as overly sweet and sickeningly courteous as the character on the old *Leave It to Beaver* show.

PLEASE,
YOU'RE WELCOME,
THANK YOU,
EXCUSE ME

# Designing Procedures

Harry Wong and Rosemary Tripi Wong (1991) note that "The number one problem in the classroom is not discipline: it is the lack of procedures and routines" (171). Procedures can be a method, process, or a set of expected behaviors for how things are to be done in the classroom. They allow students to learn, be successful, and to function effectively. Teachers must take responsibility to make the learning environment safe and secure. By creating standards, patterns, and procedures, they can better ensure that there will be minimal ambiguity, frustration, or confusion for the students. With a little forethought, you can outline the most basic classroom procedures and create systems that will be simple to implement. Later, with the students' help, you can create additional procedures as the need arises. The list of procedures is your go-to system that helps your students know what default behavior they should at least try in certain situations.

Most often when a teacher has asked me to observe and give feedback on a classroom lesson, the most common problems are related to procedures and processes, not the content of the lesson itself. When a teacher says something as seemingly benign as "Okay, class, hand in your work," students will respond in a variety of ways. Some may start shouting things out: "Wait, I'm not done!" "Can we turn it in after lunch?" "Do I have to copy it over?" "What should we do if it's not here?" Other students might move. John immediately starts walking toward the teacher, paper in hand. Emily gets up and starts collecting other students' papers, grabbing some from their desks, provoking angry reactions. Jason immediately gets out of his seat and goes over to Dylan's table to copy the last answers onto his own paper. Marcus uses the teacher's distraction by all this as an opportunity to run to the back and get a drink of water and take a quick look out the window. What should have been a simple request with an organized, respectful response becomes a few moments of chaos and a huge waste of time.

If the teacher had established a procedure for turning in papers, introduced it on the first day of class, modeled it, and asked students to rehearse it until it became routine, the chaos and confusion might have been avoided entirely. Following is a possible procedure for the preceding scenario.

THE NUMBER ONE PROBLEM IN THE CLASSROOM IS NOT DISCIPLINE: IT IS THE LACK OF PROCEDURES AND ROUTINES.

—HARRY WONG AND ROSEMARY TRIPI WONG

## Procedures for Handing in Work at the Same Time

- ☆ Hand in whatever amount you have completed at the time.
- ☆ If you don't have it at all, put your name on a blank paper with the title of the missing assignment and hand it in.
- ☆ Write concerns or questions at the top of the work.
- ☆ Stay seated, and quietly pass the work to your table leaders.
- ☆ Table leaders organize the papers, put them in the team folder, and place it in the file at the back counter.

Well-designed procedures for various activities allow for several different activities to be going on at the same time, which is imperative if you are orchestrating multiage classrooms or learning environments that encourage choice, movement, centers, and so on. Procedures can also help ensure that transitions take place efficiently, with a minimum of wasted time and confusion.

No procedure will work, however, if you don't take time to teach it to students and give them opportunities to apply their understanding of the procedure. We want students to know how to assess each situation in the classroom and, in essence, to choose the correct set of behaviors for the activity. We must understand a little about how the brain stores the information and later how it would select that set of procedures to use.

NO PROCEDURE WILL WORK IF YOU DON'T TAKE TIME TO TEACH IT TO STUDENTS AND GIVE THEM OPPORTUNITIES TO APPLY THEIR UNDERSTANDING OF THE PROCEDURE.

## How the Brain Uses Procedures

The brain is an incredible pattern-seeking instrument, constantly trying to find some order in the chaos. Leslie Hart (1998) emphasizes the brain's propensity for searching the environment for cues and clues to make sense of an experience. When the brain notices a symbol, an action, or something it has a memory of and prior experience with, then it begins to implement a program it has stored that will be an efficient, and hopefully appropriate, response. A program can be described as a series of related actions that can be triggered and to which one does not have to consciously attend, much like a line of dominoes that fall in a quick, almost unstoppable system when the first one is pushed. Recent brain research indicates that these programmed responses might actually be whole columns of nerve dendrites that fire in a pattern when triggered (Sylwester 1995).

Hart (1998) refers to this whole process as the "program implementation cycle." About this cycle, he notes that "We select the most appropriate program from those stored in the brain to deal with what is happening at the time" (158). He notes some apparent steps the brain takes in implementing a program:

☆ Evaluate: You must reasonably and accurately evaluate the situation or need (detect and identify the pattern or patterns in the environment); otherwise you simply do not know what the problem or task is.

☆ Select: You can choose and select only from those patterns and programs with which you are already familiar and already possess. If there is no frame of reference from which to draw, then you do not know what action will be appropriate. You simply do not know what to do.

☆ Implement: You cannot implement a program unless given a chance to do so. If the implementation isn't a total success, then after feedback, you must have another chance to select and implement a different, perhaps appropriate, program (158).

When you have a chance to utilize an evaluate-select-implement system, and you have a great many that work well, your confidence in implementing such programs and in yourself rises.

Creating simple procedures for the classroom, teaching them, and giving students chances to implement them give students a set of familiar programs that they can use as a part of their go-to system when they approach classroom tasks. The goal is to create routines by teaching and allowing students to practice their own programs. When students evaluate activities, select the appropriate procedures, and implement them automatically (that is, without prompting or supervision), then you know that the procedure is a habit or a stored program in their brains.

WHEN STUDENTS EVALUATE ACTIVITIES, SELECT THE APPROPRIATE PROCEDURES, AND IMPLEMENT THEM AUTOMATICALLY (THAT IS, WITHOUT PROMPTING OR SUPERVISION), THEN YOU KNOW THAT THE PROCEDURE IS A HABIT OR A STORED PROGRAM IN THEIR BRAINS.

Wong and Wong (1991) contend that there are a few reasons why students do not follow procedures. The main reason is that they do not know the specific procedure for a particular task. They perhaps have not had a discussion or an opportunity to personalize the procedure; that is, they have not been trained to follow the procedures by practicing and role-playing. Most importantly, the Wongs believe that teachers have not really thought through what happens in the classroom and taken time to create procedures for the basic activities.

Pat Belvel (1992), a classroom leadership trainer in California, believes that procedures are an important part of setting up the parameters of expected behaviors: "Once determined, classroom procedures clearly define and establish the social parameters necessary for the specific activity in behavioral, positive language" (59). I have used Belvel's recommendation to develop the following procedures.

## Well-Designed Procedures Should Do the Following

*be unique to each type of activity*

*describe social behaviors needed for the specific activity*

*be clearly defined and positively phrased*

*include behaviors that can be observed*

*involve students in formulating*

*be reviewed prior to activity*

*help maintain consistency*

*provide students with a sense of security*

A wide variety of tasks, activities, and transitions demand that you design procedures. Think through what behaviors you expect your students to follow in each situation:

*morning*

*class moving outside*

*transitions in the classroom*

*gatherings and class meetings*

*student seating*

*independent work*

*collaborative group work*

*going to lunch*

*movement of materials and papers*

*use of supplies*

*getting teacher help*

*student classroom jobs*

*use of restrooms*

*quieting a class*

*silent reading or work time*

*dismissal*

IF YOU FIND THAT YOU HAVE MORE THAN FIVE OR SIX STEPS IN A PROCEDURE, YOU MIGHT WANT TO REEXAMINE IT TO DETERMINE IF YOU HAVE ACTUALLY COMBINED TWO PROCEDURES.

Write procedures as briefly as possible, in positive language. If you find that you have more than five or six steps in a procedure, you might want to reexamine it to determine if you have actually combined two procedures. For example, you may have a procedure for silent reading after lunch that includes steps for entering the room, quieting down, getting a book, and finding a place to read. You actually have the steps for entering the room and getting settled in with the procedure for silent reading, and you will want to separate the two. One question to ask yourself is, "Are these steps all exclusive to this activity, or will there be other times when I want students to follow some of them?" The following questions can be answered within the steps of procedures:

☆ How do I want students to work together?

☆ How do I want students to work independently?

☆ How do I want students to communicate? (Silently? In 12-inch voices? Not at all?)

☆ How do I want students to use their time while on a task or at a center?

☆ How do I want students to use their time when they are finished with a task? (free choice or reading only)

☆ How do I want students to situate themselves? (in own seats or small groups)

☆ How do I want students to use or get materials they need?

☆ How do I want students to get help from other students or me?

Following is a collection of procedures for a variety of activities. You can use them as they are, alter them to meet your needs, or throw them out completely and design your own from scratch. I mean them to serve only as guidelines. I developed some myself, and some were procedures the Monarch Community School developed to implement schoolwide.

### ▶ *Reading Circle Procedures*

- ✦ Bring pencil, learning log, book.
- ✦ Sit in designated seat.
- ✦ Put date on new page in log.
- ✦ Use whisper voice to practice vocabulary and spelling words.

### ▶ *Direct Instruction*

- ✦ Listening; no talking.
- ✦ Raise hand to participate.
- ✦ Stay put.

### ▶ *Morning Routine (Primary)*

- ✦ Greet teacher and one another.
- ✦ Take off jacket.
- ✦ Sign in on chart.
- ✦ Empty backpack.
- ✦ Place lunch bag in basket or lunch card in pocket.
- ✦ Go to morning choice center.

### ▶ *Completed Math Work*

- ✦ Put work in basket.
- ✦ Choose math activity from list.
- ✦ Begin activity immediately.
- ✦ Work alone.

## ▶ *DEAR Time*

- ✦ Get book or reading materials (approved list only)
- ✦ Sit where you wish (no counters, cupboards, closet)
- ✦ Rotate groups for rockers and beanbag chairs; check schedule

## ▶ *Getting Teacher Help*

- ✦ Ask three, then me.
- ✦ Put name on "Help, please" list.
- ✦ Come to me if in a panic.

## ▶ *Monarch Co-Ed Bathroom Procedures*

- ✦ Door stays closed when not in use.
- ✦ Knock twice and wait for response.
- ✦ Respond with "Uno Momento!"
- ✦ Boys: Lift seat, *please!*
- ✦ Wash and dry hands.
- ✦ Wipe off sink.
- ✦ Leave everything *clean and ready for next person!*

## ▶ *Monarch Outside Play Procedures*

- ✦ Bounce balls against big wall only.
- ✦ Stay in fenced area.
- ✦ Throw balls only, not rocks and dirt.
- ✦ Walk around and up the ramps.
- ✦ Climb on structures only, not railings.
- ✦ Adults must supervise playing on the cement pipe.
- ✦ Respect our beautiful trees! Climb on the base of the big tree only.

### Make a PB and J

To give students practice in writing steps before involving them in writing classroom procedures, ask them to write out the steps for making a peanut butter and jelly sandwich. To make it even more fun, ask one pair of students to do a presentation to the class. One student is the director and sits in a place where she cannot see the sandwich maker. The sandwich maker stands in front of the class with all the ingredients and must do only what the director says. If the director says, for example, to get the peanut butter out of the jar and spread it on the bread, the sandwich maker must use his hands because he wasn't told to pick up a knife first. This game really helps students figure out that procedure steps must be clear and complete. Younger children can draw the steps in an illustrated flowchart.

### Brainstorming Rules

Older children love collaborating on a group list of *all* the miscellaneous classroom rules they have had over the years. You will probably be amazed at what things they remember. This activity will most likely take some time, but when they are done, students will have a huge list that you can ask them to categorize. From these categories, work as a class to write general rules or standards that encompass the little rules. I've actually had students narrow the list until the only thing they said needed to be posted as a standard was "Show *respect*." It really does cover it all, doesn't it?

## *Where to Begin*

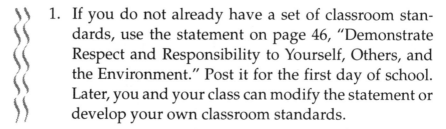

1. If you do not already have a set of classroom standards, use the statement on page 46, "Demonstrate Respect and Responsibility to Yourself, Others, and the Environment." Post it for the first day of school. Later, you and your class can modify the statement or develop your own classroom standards.

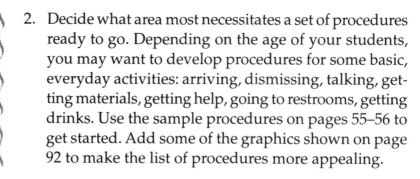

2. Decide what area most necessitates a set of procedures ready to go. Depending on the age of your students, you may want to develop procedures for some basic, everyday activities: arriving, dismissing, talking, getting materials, getting help, going to restrooms, getting drinks. Use the sample procedures on pages 55–56 to get started. Add some of the graphics shown on page 92 to make the list of procedures more appealing.

# 4

# Community and Inclusion

*Building Positive Social Interactions*

## Begin with the Brain

*The brain's capabilities are enhanced by positive social interactions. One's own identity and the ability to learn are profoundly influenced by noncompetitive, interpersonal relationships and one's feelings of inclusion in a social group.*

When you organize collaboration opportunities properly, you give single learners a great asset. When we work cooperatively with a group toward a common goal, our brain releases neurotransmitters that are related to pleasure and enjoyment. The brain also responds to immediate feedback. When interacting with others, the group provides feedback so that students can evaluate their own ideas and behaviors, and begin to modify them as necessary. By actively processing experiences with others, learners can internalize information in personally meaningful and coherent ways. With time and repeated interactions, the groups will eventually build emotional connections and a sense of community.

# Teaching Prosocial Behaviors

For the last fifteen years, every educational reform movement, restructuring document, standards guide, or new curriculum strategy has recognized and included the recommendation that students have opportunities to learn prosocial behaviors. It is obvious that our survival depends upon our young people's capacity for cooperation, interdependence, conservation, and respect for others. It's been said that the "Me" generation may well be recognizing the need to help create a "We" generation. Many educators believe that the ability to work in groups, participate in democratic planning, and maintain caring social support groups and communities will be the key to success in the twenty-first century. By experiencing and learning group participation and communication skills early on, our young people will be able to develop into resilient, caring, cooperative adults. The research also shows that academic achievement will improve as the teaching strategies include more collaborative learning experiences within a caring community of learners.

What is a "community of learners"? Alfie Kohn (1996) believes it is a place in which students feel cared about and are encouraged to care about one another. They are able to experience a sense of being valued and respected. They feel connected to one another and the teacher, and most importantly, they feel physically and emotionally safe. DiGiulio (1995) echoes these ideas and adds, "Inclusion in a prosocial classroom means that students see and are inclined toward a common good—the good of others in addition to their own individual good. They learn how to live with one another and how to be part of a group. They learn how to get their needs met, but not at the expense of others" (29). Successful learning and heightened, realistic self-esteem strongly support providing opportunities for students to work in a variety of groups and collaborate on process, products, decisions, and tasks. As Jeanne Gibbs (1998) notes, "The system of long-term membership in the Tribes process [en]sures support for all members within each small group and within the classroom. This *intentionally* created environment supports development and achievement for students of all abilities" (75). Such benefits are the result of any intentionally created group system.

> Jeanne Gibbs started the Tribes program nearly twenty-five years ago. Many educators recognize it as an exemplary educational program. Tribes defines its primary mission as "to [en]sure the healthy development of every child so that each has the knowledge, skills and resiliency to be successful in our rapidly changing world" (Gibbs 1995, 22). The Tribes process requires that a group stay together for an entire year: "A major difference between Tribes and some of the other classroom group methods is that people maintain membership in the same group for an extended period of time. This is based on research indicating that people perform better on learning tasks when they are members of 'high cohesion' rather than 'low cohesion' groups; and students who feel comfortable with their peers utilize their academic abilities more fully than those who do not" (75).

IF STUDENTS FEEL INCLUDED IN A CLASSROOM AND SEE THEMSELVES AS PART OF MULTIPLE SUPPORT GROUPS, THEY IMMEDIATELY FEEL A SENSE OF SECURITY AND EMPATHY. THEY CAN ALSO DRAW ENERGY, ASK FOR FEEDBACK, AND RECEIVE ENCOURAGEMENT FROM A GROUP OF PEERS WHEN THEY FEEL OVERWHELMED.

A wide variety of grouping strategies for the classroom exists. Children can and should see themselves as members of multiple circles. Teachers might organize minigroups according to student interest, ability, projects, research, or social alliances. These minigroups may change regularly or have benchmark criteria for changes such as age, performance, and competencies. In multiage classrooms, flexible and multiple groupings may well be a key to success.

Your goal is to create a brain-compatible environment, a place that promotes positive interactions while keeping students from minimizing their capabilities by having to deal with fear, threat, and frustration. If students feel included in a classroom and see themselves as part of multiple support groups, they immediately feel a sense of security and empathy. They can also draw energy, ask for feedback, and receive encouragement from a group of peers when they feel overwhelmed.

Orchestrating systems for group development and for community building takes a little time, but it has a great pay-off for your students and you. Taking part in a variety of groups can be a major portion of the learning interactions throughout the day, or in the beginning you may make a decision to use the groups for only certain situations. Understanding the various types of groups can give you choices as to how you might implement them. You must also begin to understand the natural developmental process that occurs when groups form and begin to work together. By designing standards for group communication, you will keep the interactions safe and productive. Robert Slavin (1994) states that students should practice cooperative learning by working in pairs or small groups at least 50 percent of their day to ensure success. Consider the following suggestions and see where you might implement more group experiences.

# Observable Patterns of a Group's Development

To orchestrate successful group experiences, you must have a basic understanding of the stages groups go through as they begin to form, bond, and create a sense of community. Most of the cooperative learning models or community building programs use the term *inclusion* to describe the first step or stage that a group must experience to be successful. Groups must then establish agreements and develop process skills. As time progresses and group members have opportunities to work on tasks and solve problems together, a community spirit and sense of caring develop among the members.

## Building Relationships, Inclusion, and Belonging

Learning to accept and trust one another in a group can occur only when the following occur:

☆ All members feel they have individual opportunities to introduce themselves and share their interests, talents, feelings, and concerns.

☆ All members can express their individual opinions, hopes, and goals without being interrupted.

☆ The group welcomes and appreciates all participants as valuable members.

☆ All members see similarities between themselves and the others in the group.

☆ All members value the group's diversity.

You should regularly orchestrate specific activities that encourage students to build relationships and create a sense of belonging. Select activities that are appropriate for the age level, interests, and length of time your students have been together. Students young and old often need a prompt or gimmick to start sharing. You might begin with simple-response questions such as the following:

☆ What's your favorite restaurant food?

☆ What's something you like to fix for yourself?

☆ What's a good movie you've seen recently?

☆ What kind of car would you like to have if money were no object?

☆ Where would you like to go for a vacation?

☆ Where in town do you like to go for fun?

☆ What is your favorite store?

Eventually, you can ask questions that generate more thoughtful responses:

☆ If I were an animal I'd be a _____
   because

☆ When I'm older I want to

☆ The last time a really felt sad was when

☆ What thing would you like to change about yourself?

The goal is to give students opportunities to share a variety of things about themselves. By sharing about themselves and listening to others, participants will begin to see similarities and feel connections. Only when group participants begin to feel as though they are a part of a group will they start to exercise their power of persuasion, influence, and compromise.

## Developing Group Processing Skills and Making Agreements

WHEN GROUPS WORK TOGETHER, THE MEMBERS NATURALLY BEGIN TO DEMONSTRATE AND PRACTICE NEGOTIATING AND COMPROMISING SKILLS.

This stage of building groups involves learning strategies that will encourage members to express diverse opinions and personal feelings without feeling judged, as well as developing basic processing skills. During this stage the group will learn effective group communication skills, various problem-solving strategies, simple and fair decision-making models, conflict-resolution and compromise methods, steps for planning and organizing, and strategies for sharing leadership. Agreeing how and when the group will work together is also appropriate for older students.

To build such processing skills, the group must have multiple opportunities to talk about and wrestle with tough ideas. Presenting them with a real-world problem or working on a simulation can give students a chance to plan as a group. When groups work together, the members naturally begin to demonstrate and practice negotiating and compromising skills. Following is a list of possible small-group discussions or tasks:

☆ The group brainstorms, discusses, chooses, and plans a theme day in which the whole class will participate.

☆ The group discusses how much television students the members' age should be allowed to watch on a school night, then makes a group recommendation.

☆ The group comes up with a new system for checking out balls during recess.

☆ The group discusses and comes up with three suggestions for ways that surplus crops from local fields might be distributed to area residents.

With time, groups who have opportunities to build relationships, work through adversity, make decisions, set goals, and experience success become ready to function truly as a team or community.

## Building a Caring Community

You'll find that your students' groups begin to demonstrate heartfelt interdependence and connection among their members. The members feel dedicated to resolving problems. The group practices skills that enable collaboration. The community celebrates its successes. This collective confidence is a wonderful thing to observe in students. To maintain the community spirit, they must build relationships through continued work and collaboration. When new people are asked to join a group, the group must begin at the first stage again to make the new member feel included.

I have seen groups who have reached a remarkable level of caring. I remember a fifth-grade girl who was experiencing an extreme family situation. As a result, she wasn't finishing her homework, and she was misplacing her schoolwork. When her teacher asked her to turn in a particular paper, she shrugged and said she hadn't done it. Her group immediately jumped up and said, "Yes you did! We saw you! Don't you remember? We were all working on it!" Two students went to her desk and rummaged around with her until they found it. They had her scribble her name quickly at the top and they handed it in for her. The student was beaming. Even though she really didn't care much about herself or her success right then, her group did care and made sure she knew it. It was just the nudge she needed.

**GOOD IDEA**

### *Team and Club Names*

Use a theme when you have students name their various groups so that you can recognize them easily. Colors, animals, and environments are always safe bets. Avoid two different types of groups (such as table teams and job committees) with similar names. Children should be able to make such statements as, "My family group is the Eagles; we meet on Fridays. My literature learning club is the Mountain Climbers, and we are reading folktales. My math skill group is the Divide and Conquer group. Right now I sit with the table group that's called Purple People Eaters!"

# Community Ground Rules and Agreements for Group Process

It's important to establish a few ground rules for how students will treat one another in their small groups and the larger community of learners. The classroom standards will certainly still serve as the basic guidelines. As you move to using group processes more in the classroom, you must determine with your students a social contract for how to interact and do your best to internalize it. The following list is a summary of basic guidelines that many successful cooperative learning models use.

### Be Attentive Listeners and Active Communicators

Give whomever is speaking your full attention without interrupting. Avoid other distractions. Use your eyes and body to focus your full attention on the speaker. Regularly share your ideas and contribute your thoughts in a way that others can hear you.

## Show Respect to Others: No Put-Downs!

This guideline ensures that each participant will avoid language or nonverbal gestures that put another person down. Demonstrate respect by keeping private things confidential when it is warranted. No gossiping about members of the group outside of the group. When group members are assured that their opinions will be respected and not put down by the others, they will be more likely to share and contribute. Even when this agreement is the only one modeled, maintained, and practiced, it changes the tone and climate of a classroom.

## Commit to Respecting Differences and Resolving Problems

Anytime people work together for extended periods of time, there will eventually be conflict and disagreement. This standard ensures that even through adversity, each member stays committed to the process and the group.

## Observe the Right to Pass

Occasionally members will choose not to respond or participate. In other words, they want the right to "pass." Everyone has the right to pass occasionally with no questions asked. If a member passes regularly or seems resistant to the group or process, then a private problem-solving discussion with you may help resolve the lack of participation.

## Share Responsibilities; Everyone Participates

This item ensures that all members agree to find ways to participate actively in the group and the process. It also reminds the strong natural leaders of a group to rein themselves in once in a while and give others a chance to see how they can contribute. Everyone needs to help with the work and responsibilities so no single member is burdened.

# Types of Groups
## Unit-Long Table Teams or Seating Groups

During a particular unit, you might group students around the particular project or research in which they are interested. These groups are short-term but still require that students adhere to the classroom standards and use the group agreements. If there is no unit of study going on or other way to logically group students, then you might want to create groups that sit together for a month.

LETTING THE GROUPS DECIDE ON A TEAM NAME IS A GREAT WAY TO HAVE THEM PRACTICE BRAINSTORMING AND DECISION-MAKING SKILLS.

Letting the groups decide on a team name is a great way to have them practice brainstorming and decision-making skills. You could assign them to come up with team names that reflect the particular unit of study. During a unit on earthworms, for example, groups might name themselves the Super Soil Shovelers, Garden Good Guys, Compost Wrigglers, Wild and Wacky Worms, or Farmers' Friends. If groups are each studying a different aspect within a unit, then they can name themselves accordingly. During an under the ground unit at Monarch one year, the groups named themselves Volcanoes, Earthquakes, Caves, Gold, and Diamonds.

## Learning Clubs

Frank Smith (1986) first described learning groups in *Insult to Intelligence.* They are comprised of students who have similar needs or interests. Students intuitively understand the criteria for membership; in other words, they know that they qualify as a member of the group. The groups may meet for instruction or to do research together, and the clubs are usually ongoing. A book club is a good example of an out-of-school learning club, and literature or novel study groups are good examples of their in-school corollaries. Students in a class who have similar reading abilities or interests might stay together throughout the year, reading novels or core literature selections. While there is no question that there is an ability level grouping going on, students also respond to being with students who have similar interests and enjoy peer group discussions and challenges.

## Skill or Ability Groups

In these groups, students are assessed and grouped based exclusively on a skill or ability level. Math skill groups and writing process groups are good examples. A key factor is that membership changes at intervals. The students don't feel locked into a group forever. At certain benchmarks in the learning or at certain times of the year, you would do another assessment and participants might change groups. Even if some students feel a stigma about being in a lower skilled group, they also are comforted by the fact that they are members of multiple groups and not just pigeon-holed into this one group.

## Year-Long Teams or Families

You can also form small groups within your class that will stay together for the whole year. They will meet regularly to work or do activities, but after the first month, they may not actually sit together in a group during regular class times. In the first few weeks of class, I let students sit where they wish and participate in various activities without assigning groups. After all students have had a chance to work with and get to know others in the class, then they are ready to participate in forming groups.

STUDENTS IN A CLASS WHO HAVE SIMILAR READING ABILITIES OR INTERESTS MIGHT STAY TOGETHER THROUGHOUT THE YEAR, READING NOVELS OR CORE LITERATURE SELECTIONS.

Students submit to me individual lists of five to seven names of students with whom they know they would work well. The lists have names of boys and girls. I emphasize that the students on the list may or may not be personal friends; they are students with whom the student knows she can work well. I also let students include on their lists the name of one person with whom they are having conflicts or someone with whom they have had conflicts and don't feel they could work. I assure students that I will try to get at least one person on their lists in the same group with them and really try not to assign the person with whom they currently have a conflict.

Now comes the tricky part. I start forming a profile of the students and their personalities, strengths, and challenges. As I sort cards, I keep in mind that profile and the group assignment guidelines (see list on page 70). I often start by distributing student leaders among the groups. I balance the leaders by distributing the disruptive or less social students among the groups. Then I add other students, keeping in mind my promise to place them with at least one of the students on their lists.

### Group Assignment Guidelines

Each group should have a balance of the following people and characteristics:

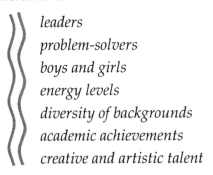

*leaders*
*problem-solvers*
*boys and girls*
*energy levels*
*diversity of backgrounds*
*academic achievements*
*creative and artistic talent*

The size of the group can vary. Many programs recommend only three or four students in a group of kindergartners or first graders. In elementary classrooms, groups of four or five work great. Groups of six or seven are more difficult to manage and are recommended only for high school or adult groups.

Make sure that the students know they will be on these teams or with these families throughout the year. They won't necessarily always sit together or work on every project together, but there will be times throughout the year when they will do things together. With the teams, schedule meetings at least once a week for them to do activities together, to discuss school events, or to make suggestions and plans for upcoming activities. The members of the teams will build almost familial bonds and begin to care about each other.

At Monarch Community School, I was the multiage intermediate teacher. The primary multiage teacher and I created family groups of five or six students that included members from first grade through sixth. The groups met every Friday for an activity, and whenever possible, they did other things together, as well. When these two buddy classes went on field trips together, they went with their family group. The students had no questions as to who was in their group. This experience with families or teams has shown me that they work *great*. The students really got to know the others in their groups, learned patience and compromising skills, as well as experienced the power and caring within the group.

### Family Teams or Extended Families

When forming year-long groups or teams, consider including the families of the team members. At back-to-school night or at family gatherings, ask the team families to sit together and get to know each other. You can even build phone trees among the teams. At open houses, group parents according to these clans to check out what each member of the team has on display. The students who don't usually have family show up feel supported and encouraged by this unique extended family. I've even seen parents start offering to pick up kids whose parents were not going to attend and bring them to school functions. "It takes a village . . . "

## Short-Term Projects

Occasionally it may make sense to create a mixed-ability group to work on a project or task. Students may request to be in a specific group. For example, to prepare for a class play, each group would take on one task: create programs, build sets, design costumes, and so on.

### Students Forming Groups

I started using this strategy with my multiage class only because I had the students for three years. I let some of the older students help create the groups based on their request cards. I would often select students who seemed to have recurring problems with whomever they were placed. I told them my criteria for balancing groups and let them go for it. They usually did a pretty good job. They also found out how difficult it can be and began to appreciate the efforts I had been making before.

## Jobs or Classroom Committees

About four times a year I recommend dividing classroom jobs and chores among committees. Tasks on which regular committees work may include caring for classroom plants; caring for class pets; creating handouts and newsletter packets; cleaning up cubbies, book shelves, and supply baskets. I have the committee meet at least once a week after a class meeting and complete their assigned task (see pages 137–38).

## *Where to Begin*

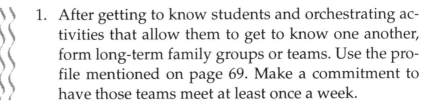 1. After getting to know students and orchestrating activities that allow them to get to know one another, form long-term family groups or teams. Use the profile mentioned on page 69. Make a commitment to have those teams meet at least once a week.

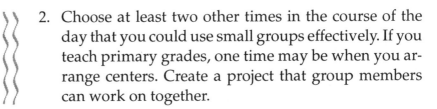 2. Choose at least two other times in the course of the day that you could use small groups effectively. If you teach primary grades, one time may be when you arrange centers. Create a project that group members can work on together.

# 5
# Meeting Students' Basic Needs

*Building Security and Fulfillment*

## Begin with the Brain

*Basic physical and psychological needs must be satisfied in order for the brain to be able to focus on complex tasks.*

The brain's first job is to maintain survival by meeting the basic physical needs of food, water, sleep, and shelter. If the brain detects a physical need, the reflex response will take over until that need is met. Consequently, poor learning has been linked to children's being hungry, tired, thirsty, and physically uncomfortable.

# Basic Human Needs

As we begin to address the importance of setting up a brain-compatible learning environment, we must also consider how students strive to get their basic needs met. In 1986, William Glasser wrote a terrific book, *Control Theory in the Classroom,* as a follow-up to his earlier books, *Schools without Failure* and *Control Theory.* In the latest work, Glasser notes, "The control theory explanation of behavior is that we always choose to do what is most satisfying to us at the time . . . Control theory is about payoff, what we need as human beings to be satisfied" (19). This theory is opposite of the stimulus-response theory that states what we do can be motivated by the people and events going on outside of us.

# Physical Needs

STUDENTS OFTEN ACT IN WAYS THAT WE DEEM INAPPROPRIATE BECAUSE THEY ARE ACTUALLY HUNGRY OR THIRSTY, OR BECAUSE THEY HAVE TO USE THE RESTROOM.

The first needs we must satisfy are physical. We must find ways to eat and drink to avoid hunger and thirst, and eventually, to ensure survival of our species, we must find ways to reproduce. We must also relieve ourselves. Many elementary students' basic hunger is not satisfied, not to mention their nutritional needs. But school is about efficiency and economy, and the idea of allowing students to eat, drink, or go to the restroom whenever they "need to" seems difficult to implement or even counterproductive to many. However, these needs are overwhelming and biological; students cannot help but seek to meet them. They often act in ways that we deem inappropriate because they are actually hungry or thirsty, or because they have to use the restroom.

Instead of helping them meet these needs, we come up with complex reward systems to try to control their behavior. Such attempts, as Kathy Checkley (1998) notes, are counterproductive: "When teachers offer students rewards, they ask them 'to forget their needs'" (6); in other words, we ask them to place gaining the rewards above their own biological needs. Checkley goes on: "Kids can do that for a while, but not for the long term" (6). We teachers must realize that, if we can orchestrate a way that students can satisfy these needs, then we will prevent other problems. We will also have far more time to spend on actually teaching and learning instead of striving to implement a reward system that works against students' best interests and drives.

## Thirst and Dehydration

The effects of thirst and dehydration on learning have been widely researched. Carla Hannaford (1995) discusses it, as does Eric Jensen (1998). Not only is dehydration linked to poor learning, but it also appears to contribute to stress levels. If some of your students' diets are salt laden, they may crave more fluids than their peers. If they drink a lot of soft drinks, coffee, or other caffeine-laden drinks to quench their thirst, then their bodies are actually in worse shape because caffeine is a diuretic. When the human body does not get enough water, the brain tells it to fulfill the need. The response to being thirsty is very clear-cut: find water, now! The problem can be complicated by the fact that children often don't realize that in fact their general discomfort is a result of thirst or even dehydration. They may not know what to ask for to feel satisfied; they just know they are uncomfortable.

NOT ONLY IS DEHY-DRATION LINKED TO POOR LEARNING, BUT IT ALSO APPEARS TO CONTRIBUTE TO STRESS LEVELS.

The FDA and other nutritional experts recommend that we all drink a lot of water. Young children should drink at least five eight-ounce glasses a day. Teenagers and adults should drink at least six eight-ounce glasses, and it's really more beneficial to drink at least eight glasses. Encourage your students to drink water throughout the day. They can drink other fluids, as well, such as juice and caffeine-free sodas, but the most healthy drink for them is water.

You might see barriers to allowing students to drink more water. What if students ask to leave the room to get drinks all of the time? If they drink a lot of water, then won't they have to use the restroom, too? Can't they take care of this at lunch and breaks???

I got over these concerns in first grade. I had recurring bladder infections, and the doctor told my mother to write a note to my teacher asking her to allow me to drink plenty of water and use the restroom as I needed. I remember the teacher announcing to the *whole* class that I was going to have this special privilege and get to drink water *whenever* I wanted to. I'll never forget the look on all of the children's faces every time I got up to go get a drink. It seemed as though they were very uncomfortable, thirsty, and jealous of my special status. Their looks made me want to find a way to sneak water back into the class! I knew in my heart even at that age that keeping children from satisfying their basic need for water was fundamentally wrong.

### Free Drinks

As long as you have class-room procedures that include getting a drink whenever a student needs one, then you shouldn't have problems with allowing it. Of course, it is more convenient if you have a sink or drinking fountain right in your classroom. One element of the procedure you'll want to include is that students not interrupt direct instruction or a student presentation. Good manners dictate that they wait until the speaker finished. However, if they are coughing, choking, or totally distracted by their thirst, encourage them to make a quick, nondisruptive jaunt to the faucet.

### Bottled Water

Have plastic water jugs filled with purified spring water (not distilled). If you have a source to help fund water delivery, try to get your hands on even the five gallon dispenser. Most often it is an inexpensive, two-and-a-half gallon jug with a spigot that sits on the counter by the sink. I've actually had various parents donate one jug per week. Sometimes I have asked students to bring in plastic mugs with names on them and have set up hooks with their names written on labels. Other times, for cleanliness, the children got paper cups with their names on them at the beginning of the day; they threw the cups away at the end of each day. Some teachers ask students to bring in their own reusable water bottles; they keep the bottles filled at their desks.

## Hunger and Malnutrition

It is equally important to meet children's need for food, and those needs are not always met. Despite the millions of dollars in free and reduced-cost breakfasts and lunches, some kids still go hungry. Children are smaller than adults, and their stomachs are smaller. They usually simply cannot consume enough food at one meal to provide the calories they need to get them all the way through to the next. Nor should we want them to. Repeated studies show that children are more likely to overeat and become overweight if we force them to eat on a schedule rather than in response to feelings of true hunger. Also, when children go through growth spurts, they may feel famished most of the time.

At Monarch Community School, a large population of students qualified for free breakfast; however, to receive it, students had to be at school at least thirty to forty-five minutes before school started. A great many of their parents didn't get them to school in time for it, for whatever reason. Kids who showed up late went to class with no food in their stomachs. The free breakfast was either packed up until the next day or thrown out if it had been prepared fresh. What a mixed-up system! I'm happy to say that, after a great deal of lobbying, we were able to serve an additional "cold" free breakfast during morning break. Many more students were able to get what they needed, which helped create an environment in which they were more likely to perform well.

IF STUDENTS SAY THEY ARE HUNGRY, DON'T ASSUME THEY ARE TRYING TO GET OUT OF DOING THE WORK AT HAND. INSTEAD, FIND WAYS TO HAVE AVAILABLE IN YOUR CLASSROOM SOME NUTRITIOUS SNACKS THAT AREN'T MESSY TO EAT.

If students say they are hungry, don't assume they are trying to get out of doing the work at hand. Instead, find ways to have available in your classroom some nutritious snacks that aren't messy to eat. Remember that young children can't always articulate their hunger needs; they often say, "I'm tired" or "I don't feel good." I usually don't even wait for a student to ask for a snack. As I get to know my students, I can often tell when they seem to have low blood sugar or lack energy. They always seem so relieved when I point out that they may be hungry. Understand that many teenagers will seem to be hungry all the time because their bodies go through so many changes during these years. I provide snacks for them, and I also give them ideas about what things they can bring in their own backpacks to help satisfy them throughout the day.

### Snack Cupboard

Keep a variety of healthy snacks in a cupboard. Individually wrapped items, although ecologically wasteful, help with portion control and cleanliness. Generic granola bars, trail mix, fruit snacks, and crackers are always the most popular items. Ask parents to donate these items. I would actually tell the parents of the children who hit the cupboard most often. They would send in a box of graham crackers now and then and express their appreciation for the opportunity to contribute. I also kept a bag of cheap red and white round star mints. With parent permission ahead of time, I would occasionally give a mint to a child who needed something to suck on or a little something sweet.

### Community Circle Snack

If class size is small enough, ask each child's family to supply snacks for the class about once every other month. We had firm guidelines at Monarch to ensure the snacks were healthy and beverages were limited to juice or water. A great primary teacher, Kris Kennedy, assigns each student to bring snacks for one week during the year. Parents decided they liked being responsible for one whole week instead of one day here and there. The students gather in a community circle and share the prepared snack. The students brought in cloth napkins that they spread out for the picnic. A parent picked up the napkins at the end of each week for laundering. The community circle is also a wonderful opportunity for students to share, chat, and have an informal, calm visiting session.

### Cough Drops, Vitamin C, and Washing Hands

During cold and flu season, many sick children come to school. As they hack away and complain of prickly throats, they spread their germs to you and the rest of the class. You can do some things to help keep the rest of the students cold and flu free.

Be sure you have students wash their hands frequently as that is the way most such viruses are spread. If you are allowed to pass out such items, I recommend you purchase huge bottles of natural, chewable vitamin C and bags of natural cough drops. You can find these items at discount warehouse stores and drugstores. If your school has strict guidelines about such things, ask parents to send them in with notes. I know many schools have very strict rules about administering anything, including cough drops and vitamins, so be sure you know your own school's guidelines. And before you or the school nurse gives them to students, be sure you get parents' permission, preferably in writing. If you are allowed to administer them, give them to students only at certain times. I kept tight limits on how many one student could have within a day, and I made sure I kept them in a place to which students did not have access. But, with proper procedures in place, the students responded beautifully. Just sucking on a vitamin or cough drop relieved some discomfort, acknowledged their illness, and provided just a bit of TLC.

## Bathroom Breaks

I believe that students shouldn't have to ask to relieve themselves. I know many schools and classrooms must adhere to rather rigid school rules regarding when students can go to the bathroom. If you implement proper procedures, including the ideal times to take breaks if they can wait, ways to do so without disturbing others, and so on, then students can simply answer the call of nature without it creating conflicts.

In a multiage fourth- through sixth-grade class, we had a single unisex bathroom in the classroom itself. Students used it much like we use the bathrooms at home—whenever they needed to go. Of course, there were occasions when students went in to work on their hair, and one student who always took a book to read while he took his time doing his business. I dealt with these problems individually; I did eventually limit their bathroom use. I recommend that you, too, make stricter standards for the few who abuse the right rather than impose rigid rules on everyone.

### Potty Passes

If your school has rigid break rules, then create potty passes that allow two students at a time to leave your classroom. I always asked students to put name cards in a pocket by the door so I knew who had left the room and where they were. You might offer students brief bathroom breaks every hour to ensure that students know they can relieve themselves when they have to.

# Psychological Needs: Belonging, Fun, Freedom, Power

Even when students' physical needs are met, they still may not be ready to learn. Glasser (1986) refers to belonging, fun, freedom, and power as essential psychological needs that drive us all. He notes, "The more students can fulfill their needs in your academic classes, the more they will apply themselves to what is to be learned . . . No class can ever be satisfying unless both teachers and students find it so" (30–31). It is quite easy to make your class satisfying in the way Glasser means.

## Belonging

To belong to a group and feel included and cared for is an important need. If your students never have the opportunity to disclose information about themselves, their families, their likes and dislikes, their concerns, then they perhaps feel judged only by their outward appearance or behavior. They can become obsessed with these two elements of themselves rather than focusing on the parts of them that truly make up who they are. Develop procedures that help students share themselves with one another; such opportunities will ensure that they get to know more about the others in the class and recognize things that they may have in common. It will help them focus on the parts of themselves that are real and important rather than just on how they look. Chapter 4 offers many ways to address this need to belong to groups and feel important and cared for by outlining ways for students to belong to many different groups within a classroom.

# Fun

Glasser points out that fun and joy are closely tied to learning. The best teachers are those who can turn learning into joyful, enjoyable experiences. Monotonous tasks don't cut it. If the learning environment gives students opportunities to play, laugh, and experience joy, then students whose need for fun is greatest (class clowns!) will have times each day to satisfy their needs.

THE BEST TEACHERS ARE THOSE WHO CAN TURN LEARNING INTO JOYFUL, ENJOYABLE EXPERIENCES.

Research shows that laughter can lower stress and perhaps even triggers the immune system to help fend off disease. A good laugh also improves memory and attention (Jensen 1996). Do you give your students the learning gift of at least one good laugh each day?

### Joke a Day

Why not have a different student share a joke every day before you begin class? Set up and maintain parameters and guidelines regarding appropriate jokes. It is also easy to sign up for an online joke service. One of the most ridiculous and most visited sites on the Internet, and yet great fun, is the Light Bulb joke web page. You can even get kids motivated about the Internet by asking them to search for jokes! If you can't really handle a joke a day, then how about a joke a week?

### Plexers and MadLibs

Include in your instruction activities that are challenging and yet demonstrate the playfulness of games and words. Plexer problems are an enjoyable way to explore word meanings, idioms, and phrases. MadLibs are a great way for a group to work together and laugh at the results.

### Theme Dress-Up Days

During class meetings or as part of an entertainment committee, students can plan a theme dress-up day. Just for fun, they select a day and dress up. Some great themes include pajama day, baby day, weird hat day, crazy hair day, and grown-up day. For even

more fun, involve the whole school. Give awards for participation and prizes for the kids who are really into it. Make the days even more hilarious by getting adults involved in the fun, too. You may feel that such days are likely to distract students, but that hasn't been my experience. Of course, you'll have to allow a little more time at the beginning of the day for the laughter and frivolity. If students have decided to award prizes, do that ceremony by the morning break so students who want to take off their costumes can do it.

### *Music and Dance*

There's nothing like a macarena or hokey pokey to bring out the silliness and clowns in a classroom. Such dances promote fun movement and playful singing. I've even taught the hustle (an old disco dance for those of you too young to remember), the electric slide, and a little stomp dance that has West Indian roots! Bring these gems out at various times to loosen things up and get people moving and laughing.

## Freedom

STUDENTS WILL POSI-TIVELY RESPOND TO A TIME EACH DAY WHEN THEY HAVE THE FREE-DOM TO CHOOSE WHAT ACTIVITY THEY WORK ON, WHAT THEY READ DURING SILENT READ-ING, OR WHAT CENTER THEY SIGN UP FOR.

Freedom, another basic need, seems almost the opposite of belonging, and to some degree, the opposite of power, as well. Even though we may seek out competition and desperately want to be included as part of a group, we also want the freedom to choose when, with whom, and for how long. The right to choose is a powerful freedom. We can observe people become quite nasty and reactive when they feel that their choices will be limited or lost all together. I rarely get to experience it these days, but I love it when I can say that I have some "free time" next week. To me that means I have the freedom to do what I want to do, to fulfill some of my wishes, goals, needs. My time isn't scheduled to meet anyone else's needs; I will have the freedom to choose, and I will experience a strong sense of satisfaction in that. When I have the freedom to choose, I don't always choose frivolous or recreational activities. I might actually feel like I have the time to begin a work project I'd been postponing.

Classroom freedom doesn't necessarily result in chaos. Students will positively respond to a time each day when they have the freedom to choose what activity they work on, what they read during silent reading, or what center they sign up for. If they complete their work, do students have freedom to choose what to do while others are finishing? By giving children a chance to be self-directed, you will be giving them a chance to experience and learn self-control. Chapter 9 offers many activities that give students choices.

## Power

The need for a sense of power over our environment, ourselves, or others is particularly difficult to satisfy, especially if you are a kid. In fact, we all almost always compete for power. Glasser (1986) suggests that almost all of us are ambitious and worry about "winning." The list of how we worry about power is endless: our need to be "right," to be recognized, to achieve and influence others, to look good, and so on. Even those people whom you know are not driven by power and are quite humble sometimes compete for who can be the most humble!

Some students feel powerless in their home environment, in situations with friends, in school. They may push hard to have this need fulfilled. The more you can give them a sense of control over themselves, the more you can help them see what is in their power, the more self-directed they become in their learning. Chapters 7 and 8 outline many ways to grant students power over areas of classroom management.

THE MORE YOU CAN GIVE STUDENTS A SENSE OF CONTROL OVER THEMSELVES, THE MORE YOU CAN HELP THEM SEE WHAT IS IN THEIR POWER, THE MORE SELF-DIRECTED THEY BECOME IN THEIR LEARNING.

## *Where to Begin*

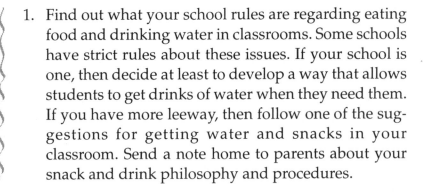

1. Find out what your school rules are regarding eating food and drinking water in classrooms. Some schools have strict rules about these issues. If your school is one, then decide at least to develop a way that allows students to get drinks of water when they need them. If you have more leeway, then follow one of the suggestions for getting water and snacks in your classroom. Send a note home to parents about your snack and drink philosophy and procedures.

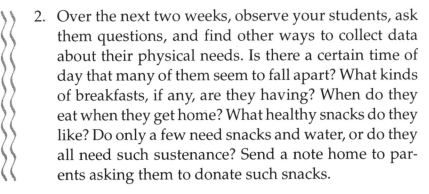

2. Over the next two weeks, observe your students, ask them questions, and find other ways to collect data about their physical needs. Is there a certain time of day that many of them seem to fall apart? What kinds of breakfasts, if any, are they having? When do they eat when they get home? What healthy snacks do they like? Do only a few need snacks and water, or do they all need such sustenance? Send a note home to parents asking them to donate such snacks.

3. Plan something fun with the students, such as Crazy Hair Day or Twin Day! Get into the spirit yourself!

# 6
# Building Curiosity

*Making Connections
and Ensuring Engagement*

## Begin with the Brain

》》 *The brain seeks to make sense of every experience. The degree to which one explores relationships and makes connections grows and changes with normal developmental stages.*

The brain's attentional system has two main purposes. It first must pay attention to ensure that survival takes place. Research has revealed that the brain pays attention to extend pleasurable states, as well. The brain is always sizing up situations to determine the possible risk involved or the pleasure that may result. This focus may shift from external input to internal clues and memories of prior experiences. Children are more likely to engage in content when they can see its connections to their real world.

# Piquing Curiosity

Brain-compatible learning environments are places where students' curiosities are piqued and potential anxiety, frustration, or confusion is diminished. In truly brain-compatible environments, you don't hear children say, "What are we gonna do now?" They already know, or they are part of the process of deciding. They have a sense of curiosity and anticipation, as well as a sense of confidence in knowing a little about what's ahead. In a well-orchestrated classroom, the students are well informed about the agenda, engaged in the process of learning, interested in the next steps, and secure about learning something new. When students are constantly asking, "What are we doing today?" you must ask yourself why they don't know.

IN TRULY BRAIN-COMPATIBLE ENVIRONMENTS, YOU DON'T HEAR CHILDREN SAY, "WHAT ARE WE GONNA DO NOW?" THEY ALREADY KNOW, OR THEY ARE PART OF THE PROCESS OF DECIDING.

*Curiosity* is defined as "an eager desire to know or learn." If students are curious, then something has probably occurred to trigger their emotions. This arousal of emotions allows their attentional system to zoom in and focus on the source. We know that attracting and holding attention is the key to learning and memory. Bob Sylwester (Margulies and Sylwester 1998) notes that, "While intellectual challenge (and even mild stress) can enhance learning, severe short-term and chronic stress shift us into a mode of operation in which we react to danger rather than think rationally about it" (9). In other words, curiosity is difficult to maintain in situations that involve fear or potential threat.

Robert Sylwester also notes that emotions can be aroused by a memory as well as by an event that might occur. Two basic emotions focus on what might occur in the future: anticipation and fear. *Anticipation* is "an expectation; a looking forward to with pleasure." *Fear*, then, would be "a looking forward to with dread." Anxiety is produced when fear blends with anticipation.

Jensen (1996) notes that children give incredible nonverbal signals about the range of emotions they are feeling. When they anticipate something, they will often open their eyes wide, lean forward, and possibly hold their breath. When children are curious, they may bring a hand up to the head, look interested, and actually tilt the head. But add something to the situation with which the child is unfamiliar or that has a fearful connection for the child, and you might observe restricted breathing, tightened muscles, and a closed body posture (121).

We speak about creating brain-compatible classrooms that are low threat, safe, and secure. Although there are some schools where children are truly in physical danger, more often children are simply anxious, confused, and frustrated by something that is occurring in the classroom. We must create sufficient interest and curiosity, without contributing to students' anxiety and fear. This delicate balance is difficult for any educator to orchestrate.

You can inspire and generate student curiosity and minimize anxiety in at least four ways:

> ☆ Point out connections between the curriculum and students' lives.
>
> ☆ Keep students informed about what is going to happen by posting agendas, calendars, schedules, and plans.
>
> ☆ Maintain optimal learning states in which students have opportunities to apply concepts and understanding to new situations; balance acceleration and new challenges with expansion of familiar material and enrichment.
>
> ☆ Provide varying stimuli regularly, and balance novelty with constancy.

## Create Personal Curriculum Connections

To promote curiosity, make it your goal to provide opportunities for students to make personal connections to what you are teaching. Young students are egocentric enough that connecting any learning to them will inevitably trigger their curiosity. And adolescent and older students, struggling to self-identify, are always questioning relevance to their own lives.

We often teach material as though we were just delivering it to students, as if their heads could be opened up and the information just poured into their brains. We feel overwhelmed at the mass of content that we are required to cover; we often charge ahead and neglect to help students see the connections to their own lives

TO PROMOTE CURIOSITY, MAKE IT YOUR GOAL TO PROVIDE OPPORTUNITIES FOR STUDENTS TO MAKE PERSONAL CONNECTIONS TO WHAT YOU ARE TEACHING.

that are so vital. When we give students a chance to see relevance by recalling a prior experience with similar materials or making an emotional connection to the curriculum, they will be able to leap in and engage! If the material is irrelevant to the student's daily life, or not focused on things that are connected to the student's real world, then the student may never engage.

You can help students connect in only two ways: by generating their memories of similar experiences and providing new first-hand experiences. Introduce new content in a way that connects it to what you hope the students already know. For example, when I begin a unit on reptiles, I discuss reptiles with my students to find out what experiences with reptiles they have had and to bring memories of those experiences to the surface. As students retrieve these memories, the emotions they experienced as they learned or interacted with reptiles emerge, as well. Such an activity creates an anticipatory set that you can use to create an atmosphere of curiosity and intrigue about the next lessons, even if they have had a negative experience with reptiles.

Even more effective is actually bringing in items for the students to observe and touch. Students are immediately interested, and their curiosity goes through the roof! Larry Lowery (1989) of U.C. Berkeley's Lawrence Hall of Science refers to firsthand experiences or dynamic simulations as being the most "powerful learning" that can occur. We must create opportunities to introduce concepts to students through hands-on experiences in class or on field trips. We are notorious for saving the field trip until the end of a unit. But if field trips lend themselves to the most powerful learning, then we should make them the starting point of the entire unit!

During the unit, include centers that have hands-on materials and resource books about the topic so that students may continue to engage and ask questions. As their curiosity is piqued, they should have support materials that allow them to dive into the content and see what else interests them. Place a stack of self-stick notes near a bulletin board for students to write their questions on; others will answer on the notes, as well.

# Keep Students Informed with Posted Agendas, Calendars, Schedules, and Plans

You can capture children's attention and curiosity by using simple agendas and calendars that tell them what is going to happen. Not knowing what will happen during the course of the day can create anxiety for many students. Posting a morning agenda can make such students involved, curious, and eager. Posting weekly schedules is also important, especially if there are certain activities students do on certain days of the week. Many teachers find that they are constantly answering such student questions as "Is today the day we go to computer lab?" "Are we going to finish our art projects today?" "Is this an early-release day?" "Are we doing PE outside tomorrow?" By the end of the day, teachers feel as though they have answered the same question twenty-five times! But just consider the internal process that was going on in the children. They were really unable to attend to the task at hand because they were either anxious or excited about the schedule.

## Morning Agendas

You will have a set of arrival procedures in place for when students arrive. They should include coming in, greeting you, putting things away, and so on. The next item should be reading or copying the daily agenda.

Post the agenda where all can see it. I prefer to use chart paper, but a white, wipe-off board will also work. By using chart paper on a stand, I ensure that students who are absent a day can go look at that day's agenda one page back. It also allows me to refer to earlier pages to see when certain activities, such as a classroom journal, were started or worked on. As students become writers, ask them to copy the agenda down into a journal or notebook. By taking time to look and then write down each item, students are able to pause and visualize what doing that item will entail. Many students will say, "Oh, yeah, I saw the agenda, looks the same as always." But after copying it down, they might say, "Hey, did you see that two more groups get to go to the computer lab today?"

I use a web for most agendas. I write with the same color pen the items that occur every day: morning gathering, recess, lunch, drop everything and read (DEAR), closing comments. Then I write in the items that will be going on during specific days in a different color and add which groups will be doing what. As often as possible, I draw a little graphic to represent the activity. I have developed a few graphic symbols that are consistent with certain activities: a pencil for writing, a book for reading, arrows or a questions mark for choice activities, several happy faces together for a class meeting (see examples on page 91). I negotiate with nonwriters or slow writers to draw the symbols and write at least one of the words (see examples on page 92).

You can also use a linear schedule. The main difference between the two is that an agenda gives a general idea of the ways chunks of time are going to be used during the day; schedules get down to the minutia and time table of the day (9:00–9:05 attendance; 9:05–9:15, calendar; 9:15–9:20 review daily schedule). I find that it's easier and saves time to do an agenda and just lump such items together into something such as "morning circle"; the students know what you do during that time. But a schedule can be particularly helpful if some of the daily activities take place at different times on different days. For instance, I've been at schools that have early lunch on Mondays, Wednesdays, and Fridays, and late lunch on Tuesdays and Thursdays. Or many schools have early release times one day a week. Post schedules with the various daily information so students don't get confused about what to do on which day.

Lunch
Time

Many primary teachers I know also make little clock faces with the time of each event. You can laminate them and either tape them or pin them next to the activity. Students are able to start telling time by matching the paper clock to the face of the clock in the room to determine when that activity will be taking place.

# Sample Morning Agendas

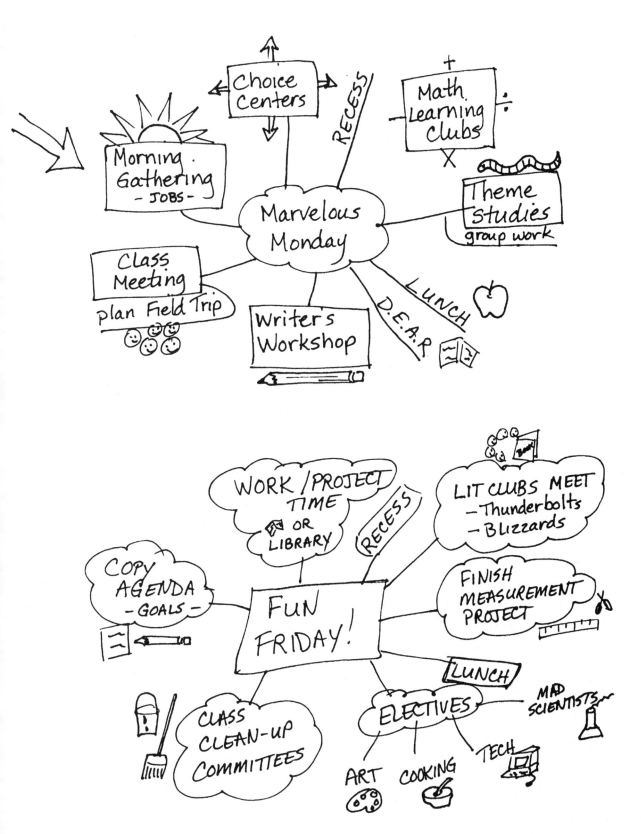

# Graphic Symbols for Procedures

You can also add a goal-setting activity to the morning agenda. Years ago I incorporated strategies suggested in the Johnsons' book *The One Minute Teacher.* After students had recorded the brief agenda in their notebooks, they had to mentally review the tasks for the day, then write down one goal for the day right under the their agenda. This practice allowed them to focus on what they wanted to have done by the end of the day, and to take responsibility for its completion. At the end of the day, students referred to the agenda, marked off the items they had completed, and circled the tasks they didn't get done. Then they would take a moment to write a sentence that indicated to what degree their written goals had been met.

## Weekly Schedules

In many brain-compatible classrooms, teachers orchestrate the curriculum around themes, and they integrate subjects accordingly. They might post weekly schedules each Monday and send copies home to alert kids and parents about the flow of the week. Students and their families may generate interest and curiosity by discussing what is coming up. I also try to label some of the lessons and interactions in clever ways that might intrigue students without necessarily giving away the exact nature of the activity. "Creepy Crawly Lab!" for example, will get kids thinking and anticipating much more than "Earthworm Experiment 3" might.

IN MANY BRAIN-COMPATIBLE CLASS-ROOMS, TEACHERS ORCHESTRATE THE CURRICULUM AROUND THEMES, AND THEY INTEGRATE SUBJECTS ACCORDINGLY.

I often provide a weekly contract for older children's notebooks. I write in the specific schedule for their group. By seeing when they will have project time or be able to use the computer, they are able to formulate a plan to manage their time for the week. A word of caution here, however: By providing a super-detailed schedule, laden with all of the assignments due and homework deadlines, you may make a student feel overwhelmed and depressed at the enormity of the expectations for the week. Make sure that agendas and schedules give basic information in a clever or creative format, but that they don't become a checklist or massive to-do list.

## Thematic Unit Web or Chart

If you are orchestrating a thematic unit for two to six weeks, take time to create a modified web or chart for the students. Highlight the major topics for each component of the unit. Include basic information about research projects or group activities. Post the field trip schedule and the date and time of the culminating learning celebration. Many children comment on not having any idea when a curriculum unit is going to end. They say that it just keeps going until the teacher's done. Knowing the scope of a unit helps these students maintain focus and interest. Of course, as the teacher you must be ready to work within a basic framework. Often a good thematic unit will run over our planned time. Include students in the modification of the schedule, and give them reasons for continuing.

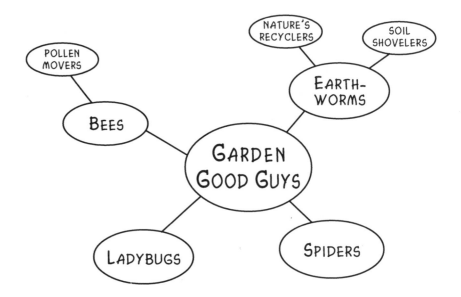

For most of my teaching career, I have used year-long thematic plans. I write them up briefly in a web and give copies to students for the front of their learning log notebooks. Parents get a copy at back-to-school night. I also post a large version in the classroom. One year I had a sixth grader join the class mid-year. He merged beautifully into the unit we were currently working on. It wasn't until later that I realized I hadn't reviewed with him our year-long plan or where we were on that time line. But he was a smart guy, and after the first week he approached me and said, "I see the year-long theme plan on the board over there. We're working on an 'under the ground' unit that we were supposed to do last month. Are we behind?" Because of the posted clues, he was able to put it all together. He later commented that he was happy we were running a little behind; he didn't want to miss anything because it all looked so interesting!

# Balance: Maintaining Optimal Learning States

Several classroom orchestration models refer to the idea of balance to maintain students' interest, curiosity, and attention, the idea of flow mentioned in chapter 1. One way you can help students enter the flow zone is to have a system in place whereby, when students get bored, they are given new feedback to inspire and encourage them. Likewise, the activity never becomes too challenging to be totally overwhelming. There are opportunities to explore and practice a given skill to prepare for a possible next challenge.

Students may demonstrate stress or resistance if constantly under pressure to accelerate upward. Eventually their curious nature will be buried under the intensity of always being pushed to the next level of competency. Many programs in which gifted students are in standard classrooms suggest that they might be able to be satisfied by lateral enrichment in a certain topic or competency level. By expanding their comprehension of the material through enrichment, they might not be so bored in a class with students who were not working at comparable levels of competency and pace.

Students probably used a form of self-directed learning to learn to ride a bike, use the computer, play a sport, or do arts and crafts projects. Use the following processes to help the learners in your classroom have optimal experiences. They set challenges and expectations high, keep the stress level low, and provide feedback and resources so that students might move on when ready. If the stimulus is there for the next step, learners will be attracted to it when they are ready.

ONE WAY YOU CAN HELP STUDENTS ENTER THE FLOW ZONE IS TO HAVE A SYSTEM IN PLACE WHEREBY, WHEN STUDENTS GET BORED, THEY ARE GIVEN NEW FEEDBACK TO INSPIRE AND ENCOURAGE THEM. LIKEWISE, THE ACTIVITY NEVER BECOMES TOO CHALLENGING TO BE TOTALLY OVERWHELMING.

## Use Novelty and Varying Stimuli

If you want to get students' attention and get them involved in a given activity, create a variety of instructional strategies to "hook" them. To get someone's attention most quickly, you need to do or provide something that contrasts to what you are already doing or what students can easily predict. You might try teaching from the back instead of the front of the classroom. Or try new seating arrangements to liven things up a bit. Play new music as students enter the room. Or turn the lights off and close the curtains to change the mood. As Jensen (1998) notes, "Overall, you'll want to provide a rich balance of novelty and ritual. Novelty ensures attentional bias, and ritual ensures that there are predictable structures for low stress" (50–51).

In certain classrooms, the teacher or a student each day hides a certain item related to the theme somewhere in the room. When students arrive the next day, even the most recalcitrant of them are immediately hooked into searching the room for the item. The activity was clearly only an attention-getting device. But if you can get their attention for a few minutes, you've won half the battle.

### (KWL) Know; Want to Know; Learn

This strategy has been around in many forms for a long time; its simplicity is the reason it works. As an introduction to a topic, ask students to brainstorm what they already *know* about it. This discussion encourages students to search for their personal connections to the topic. Then generate questions as to what the students *want to know.* At the end of the unit, review the questions and ask students to record what they *learned*—a simple, yet tried-and-true strategy for triggering curiosity.

### Mystery Box

This strategy works especially well in primary classrooms, but don't underestimate its power in upper levels, as well. Wrap an old box with a removable lid with wrapping paper. Place an object or a piece of paper with the name of an object or animal written

on it in the mystery box. Students play twenty questions. Generating only yes-or-no questions, they try to guess what is in the box. They must guess within twenty questions. Help children see what kinds of questions will be most helpful.

### Countdown

If there is a special day coming up, put the number of days left until the event up on the board. We had a day to celebrate division, and the countdown said, for example, "D-Day: 13 days left." This kind of daily check-in serves as a reminder and builds interest and anticipation.

## Where to Begin

1. Post a daily agenda for all to see. Make it an extremely simple web with symbols or a linear schedule. Give your students and yourself a chance to review the agenda at the beginning of the day, and use it to recapitulate at the end.

2. Go through your lesson plans and choose at least five for which you can easily note personal, relevant connections for your students. Don't leave it up to chance for your students to make the connections! Create a door into the lesson by having an informal discussion with the class that gets them talking about what this concept has to do with them. Create hooks!

# 7
# Managing Conflicts and Solving Problems

*Strategies for Resolution*

SHE'S BUGGING ME AGAIN!

## Begin with the Brain

⟩⟩ *Positive social interactions can enhance and influence our experiences. A safe and secure emotional climate that promotes strategies for resolving conflicts is a key to successful learning.*

Social situations can be stressful for many students. Students' roles within a classroom or status among children can influence the brain's chemistry, causing it to release stress hormones in certain situations. Being able to understand what is going on in the brain and body during a conflict may help students manage their emotions and enhance their ability to seek appropriate resolutions. As students experience strategies for solving problems successfully, their self-esteem and confidence increase. Understanding how to manage emotional upsets is a basic coping skill for life.

# Reducing Conflicts

If we know that the brain responds to perceived threats in the environment in a way that may impair some students' ability to learn, then we must create systems that can reduce the likelihood of conflicts between or among the students. You can implement systems, such as those described in chapters 2, 3, and 8, to prevent such conflicts. You must also create systems for dealing with conflicts that do occur; such systems will include strategies to resolve and solve problems, ways to manage student upsets, and models for building consensus to ensure that all feel included in the decisions.

People usually have problems due to the following:

### *Stuff*

*possession of an item; ownership*

*inequality of distribution; having less than others*

*missing items; loss or suspected stealing*

*destroyed property, broken by accident or on purpose*

*lack of materials; not having what is needed*

### *Needs*

*feeling excluded from a group or abandoned*

*loss of friends or colleagues; loneliness*

*lack of power or leadership*

*fear of losing; competition*

*lack of essentials to meet basic needs: food, water, rest, fun, shelter*

### *Identity or Values*

*disrespect shown toward family*

*disregard of or disrespect for ethnicity*

*stereotype of cultural background*

*disrespect of personal goals*

*lack of acceptance for ideas*

*put-down of physical characteristics*

In brain-compatible, learner-centered environments, the students not only know some reasonable strategies for preventing conflict, but they also have a plan for dealing with any conflicts that may arise. Such knowledge gives students a sense of security that allows them to feel comfortable taking risks and participating fully with other students in the classroom. You and your students will be amazed at the sense of community that develops from these agreements, and students lucky enough to experience this kind of environment will be empowered to create and abide by these kinds of agreements in other situations. Learning the skills for avoiding, preventing, and resolving conflicts will help them throughout their lives.

### *Urging Messages*

This activity is a clear format for sending statements to others in small or large groups. Encourage students to think of something they would like to urge another person to do, keep doing, or stop doing. For example, "Robert, I urge you to keep eating lunch with me every day"; "Jason, I urge you to control your humming when you are working, because it makes it hard for me to concentrate"; "Lynnette, I urge you to come play handball with us at morning recess." The other student doesn't need to respond. This activity is good to do at morning gatherings, during class meetings, or at end-of-the-day closures. As the facilitator, be sure to limit just how many urging messages any one student can say or receive in a day. Encourage a variety of statements; some will be requests, some, compliments, and others, constructive criticisms. Be sure to model the activity yourself by sending a few urging messages each day.

ESTABLISHING CLASS-ROOM STANDARDS AND PROCEDURES ARE PREREQUISITES FOR ANY LEARNER-CEN-TERED CLASSROOM.

# Preventative Strategies
## Standards and Procedures

As I say in chapter 3, establishing classroom standards and procedures are prerequisites for any learner-centered classroom. Make sure that the standards you select are clear, basic, assertive, and meaningful. On the first day in class, create a motto that reflects standards of behavior. For example, you and your students might come up with "All members of this class will demonstrate respect and responsibility to themselves, others, and the environment." With your students, restate, interpret, and discuss this motto to make sure that *all* students clearly understand its broad meaning. Post it with the rest of your classroom standards so you and your students can refer others to it.

When students know what the expected behaviors are and have a chance to practice them successfully, they are more likely to follow them on a regular basis. Review appropriate procedures prior to each activity until the students have internalized the pattern and programmed it into their brains. When the behavior is stored as a program, the brain doesn't need to use much conscious effort to enact the steps; it's as if it were on automatic pilot. When most students in the class demonstrate these positive behaviors, conflicts and disruptions will be greatly reduced.

## No Put-Downs

Put-downs are disrespectful words or actions that make someone else feel mad, humiliated, embarrassed, frustrated, or sad. Jeff Caplan (1997), director of the Santa Cruz–based Common Language for Education and Resolution (CLEAR), defines put-downs: "Put-downs are anything someone says or does that makes someone else feel mad or sad. [They] include literal statements like 'You're so stupid!' sub-literal put-downs like 'Oh, yeah, you're my best friend!' said with a sarcastic voice, and nonverbal gestures, facial expressions and mimicry . . . How do I know if it's a put-down? A put-down is defined by the person who receives it. For example, if you say, 'Why are you wearing that tee shirt?' to your best friend, it might not feel like a put-down. If you said the same words to someone whom you didn't know so well, it might feel like a put-down to them." In other words, the person to whom the words or actions are directed is the one who determines whether or not they are a put-down. How, then, do we define and deal with put-downs every day?

**TURN YOUR CLASS-ROOM INTO A PUT-DOWN–FREE ZONE.**

Turn your classroom into a put-down–free zone. It takes time, but it's well worth it. To begin, demonstrate just how pervasive verbal and nonverbal put-downs are in our language and culture. Do this simple activity with your students. Videotape a five-minute segment of a popular TV sitcom the humor in which depends on put-downs. After reviewing what put-downs sound like and what nonverbal put-downs look like (eye-rolling, looking away, arms folded and head cocked to one side), show the video clip. Ask students to tally the number of put-downs they observed in the clip. On a clip I used, my middle school students found more than forty in less than five minutes! Put-downs permeate our culture so that we become almost desensitized to them, often letting them slide by without commenting.

Give students strategies for dealing with put-downs that don't allow them to engage in the same behavior. Figure out systems to make your students more aware of how often they are using put-downs to put themselves up.

What should students do if they hear put-downs? A simple response that Caplan recommends is to say, "That felt like a put-down. Could you say it in a different way?"

You can expand the put-down–free zone to your entire school. Doing so means introducing the rules to the rest of the staff and creating some agreements about not using put-downs yourselves. If the staff cannot live without put-downs during staff meetings, how can you expect children to demonstrate this common courtesy?

### Put-Down Paper Doll

Occasionally, if a class is having difficulty giving up put-downs, I have tried this activity. Cut a large figure of a person out of butcher paper, and ask students to use pens and crayons to draw on the features of a generic person. Over a week or so, note every time students put other students or themselves down. Either the person who put another down or a volunteer tears off a small piece from the paper person to illustrate that every time we hear ourselves put down, we lose a bit of ourselves. This visual aid can be powerful, and it really helps students get the idea of the damage put-downs can do over time. Some teachers added another element: as members of the class do things to encourage and support others, they are allowed to replace the torn-away bits.

## Essential Agreements: Social Contracts

Essential agreements are usually verbal contracts that people make about how they will talk, act, and behave with each other. They are different from rules in that they don't have consequences tied to them. Such agreements can be very informal, such as when I ask someone to please interrupt me if I've told a story before. That person might otherwise follow common social courtesies and *not* interrupt, perhaps even feigning interest over an already-heard story. Essential agreements and social contracts with friends, relatives, business associates, and students about how we would like them to talk, act, and behave in certain situations help relationships by letting others know what boundaries are important to us.

You might start with social agreements about put-downs. For many years, Susan Kovalik and her associates would say "Ding-a-ling!" if we heard something we perceived as a put-down. In my classroom, we simply said "Ding!" Of course, we didn't mean the phrase to be *another* put-down; it was supposed to represent a bell going off to alert the speaker that the statement was considered a put-down. The person who said the put-down would usually immediately apologize and set the record straight by restating the sentence in a positive way. Sometimes younger children have to hear positive options for making certain statements. They can learn to help others restate feelings in positive ways, without using put-downs. I also emphasized that, since we had an essential agreement regarding put-downs, anyone who heard a put-down had the *responsibility* to help classmates restate their feelings in more positive ways. After implementing this procedure regarding no put-downs, you might hear conversations like the following:

Alex: *Oh, no, burritos for lunch! They're so stupid!*
Katie: *Ding, Alex, Ding!*
Alex: *Well, they are. I hate them.*
Katie: *Then say that without putting them down, 'cause I like them.*
Alex: *I wish we weren't having burritos. I really don't like them.*

Once students understand that agreement, you might add essential agreements or social contracts that deal with how students refer to the grown-ups on campus. Some schools allow students to call teachers by their first names if the teachers feel comfortable with that. Other schools insist students call teachers by "Mr." or "Ms." So-and-so. Many agreements involve polite language. Are "please" and "thank you" part of the students' everyday language? Or what will you do when students interrupt adults? Under what circumstances is it okay? One teacher I know says that the 3 Bs are the only appropriate reasons to interrupt her: blood, bruises, or barf.

In most cases, the teacher establishes the agreements and social contracts within the classroom. Doing so sets a general tone and gives students boundaries for interactions with each other, something that is especially important in secondary classrooms. As the teacher, establish your needs and preferences first, then make agreements and contracts with students about how everyone will treat one another.

Following is a list of possibilities for which establishing essential agreements and social contracts may prove helpful:

> *the words students will use to refer to one another and to you*
> *saying* please, thank you, *and* you're welcome *when asking for or receiving something*
> *ways to respond to put-downs*
> *borrowing something with or without asking*
> *appropriate times and manners in which to interrupt a conversation*
> *the degree of casual dress that will be accepted*
> *guidelines for how students will treat furniture*
> *guidelines for establishing acceptable seating positions*

## Class Gatherings

Class gatherings are perfect opportunities for you and your students to express feelings, share ideas, build inclusion, and prevent possible conflicts that seem to be developing. These whole-class conversations are usually informal but regular and frequent gatherings in the morning or at the end of the day. They may be a brief check-in at the beginning of class in a secondary classroom. Sometimes students share or report on a special activity they're going to get to do. Minor problems might be solved using an "urging message" (see description on page 100). These gatherings are also the perfect opportunity for you and students to share compliments or praise others for recent accomplishments. They are wonderful community activities that build relationships, and you can use them for closure and reflection at the end of the day.

## Class Meetings to Prevent Problems

Class meetings are more formal and are usually scheduled just once a week. Establish specific procedures and tools, such as talking sticks and agendas for these meetings (see additional ideas in chapter 8). You might train some students to be facilitators, recorders, and timekeepers. In class meetings, your class discusses potential problems and makes decisions ahead of time to avoid possible conflicts.

For example, in one such meeting, students mentioned that several recess balls were missing. They anticipated that pretty soon there would be a conflict over who got to play with the few remaining balls. They made a proposal to send several students to other classes to search for the missing balls and to set up a sign-out system that would guarantee that students all had fair opportunities to play with the remaining equipment. As students see the effectiveness of the preventative strategies, they use them more often and avoid having to use problem-solving strategies later.

# Increasing Motivation

Most positive discipline models and brain-based classroom management systems will give many reasons why educators should avoid extrinsic rewards. If it's not the punishment-consequence system ("Do this or here's what will happen to you"), it's the reward system ("Do this and you'll get . . . ") that is at the heart of many classroom management systems. Alfie Kohn (1996) says,

"Rewards work very well to get one thing, and that thing is temporary compliance" (32). Reward systems can actually insult and damage the caring, democratic community of learners that has been feeling intrinsic satisfaction from doing the right things.

Although some incentives may provide momentary fun, they still can send a wrong message: Do the right thing and you will get a reward. Instead, students should understand that classroom standards and courtesies are expected. They don't have a choice about behaving that way. As DiGiulio (1995) says, "Never materially reward students for cooperating, for respecting others, or for taking good care of their own bodies" (121). That being said, I do know that on a practical day-to-day basis, I have seen tangible incentives with immediate pay-offs used effectively to motivate students. Let's face it, sometimes we really need temporary compliance! Many children are already so dependent on extrinsic motivation that they may respond to little gimmicks in the classroom in a big way. Some children, especially older ones, actually may need to be weaned off of a reward system if that is how they have been made to comply in the past. I have challenged them for just a day, or a maximum of a week, with little incentives (extra PE time, free choice time, a video, even a pizza party) and made the expectations very clear. I've had these little challenges for cleaning up the room for open house, staying in at recess to finish projects, having all work packets in before noon on Friday, going without *any* conflicts all day. I do not challenge students to upset them or make them anxious, but to put a little pressure on all of us to see if we can "beat the clock." I feel the use of these motivators, especially when I am confident that we have a 90 percent chance of success, can encourage all of us to kick into gear a little. Incentives, when used sparingly and wisely, can still be motivational techniques.

I do recognize the wisdom in what Kohn (1996) says. The more we use bribes and threats to control people, the more we feel we must control them because they grow accustomed to doing what someone else tells them or to rebelling. It takes time and effort to help students find their own reasons to act responsibly and generously. So I use short-term motivational strategies that involve incentives only under the following conditions:

REWARDS WORK VERY WELL TO GET ONE THING, AND THAT THING IS TEMPORARY COMPLIANCE.
— ALFIE KOHN

☆ The students are dependent on a reward system and extrinsic motivators, and they need some time to make the transition to intrinsic satisfaction.

☆ I need immediate but temporary compliance from the students so they can complete a task or behave in a certain way.

☆ I set up a one-time only wager that playfully challenges students to complete a task or behave in a certain way.

☆ I am totally stressed out and need temporary compliance to get through the day!

I always follow Jane Nelsen and Lynn Lott's (1994) parameters, though: "A friendly, challenging bet may help motivate teens to learn life skills . . . To be effective, the bet must be made with a friendly, respectful, playful attitude . . . You can make a bet with your teens without controlling them" (189).

## Resolution Strategies

### Maintaining Standards and Agreements Consistently

When you make an agreement with your students, everybody involved must be committed to maintaining its integrity and purpose. As the teacher-facilitator of the class, you need to build trust by establishing your dedication to doing so. If you or the students have taken time to create a social contract, everyone should also agree to uphold the ideals within the agreement. Unfortunately, such trust usually means that, in the beginning, you will be the watchdog. If you remain consistent, however, students will begin to demonstrate their commitment to the agreement, as well. The brain interprets consistent behavior as security, something that can be counted on, and your consistent behavior will promote the feeling of relaxed alertness in the classroom.

If you and your students agree that no one should put feet on the desk, for example, then you must consistently notice when students are not following this standard. In the beginning, *every time* you see someone casually place feet up on a desk, you must make an observational comment in a calm, assertive, neutral voice: "We

WHEN YOU MAKE AN AGREEMENT WITH YOUR STUDENTS, EVERYBODY INVOLVED MUST BE COMMITTED TO MAINTAINING ITS INTEGRITY AND PURPOSE.

107

agreed that putting your feet up on the desks isn't a (good, healthy, respectful, attractive) thing in our class." You will make the statement regardless of who the student is, even if the student was absent on the day the agreement was made.

The key here is to be a watchdog for only two to three agreements each week. If you have a ton of agreements, it will become tedious to monitor all of them. Recruit other students to give respectful reminders about other agreements. In some cases, the behaviors are just old bad habits, and you and your students will need time to begin to change the behaviors until the more positive behaviors become routine. You can make additional agreements to uphold the other agreements by speaking up and mentioning it to the person who needs reminding.

It's important to avoid embarrassing students, so occasionally, I will have private conversations with students who are having a hard time remembering the agreements. We discuss ways they would like me to remind them during class or when in front of other students. We have even worked out secret signals. One class decided that, during times when many of us were suffering from colds, it was annoying and disgusting to have others constantly sniffling and snorting. We also decided that, if you had to blow your nose hard, you should step outside or into a restroom; no one wanted to hear or witness this bit of personal hygiene. Instead of asking someone to "go blow your nose," though, we decided that someone who heard another student sniffling a lot would simply get a tissue and kindly hand it to the sniffler as a respectful reminder.

When one or more students break an agreement more than once, a good strategy for confronting them is to use the following prompts:

☆ "We agreed that (state the agreement)."

☆ "I saw (heard, noticed) that you (state the behavior)."

☆ "Help me understand why you didn't stick to the agreement" or "Help me understand what caused you to break the agreement."

☆ "What can we do to reestablish the agreement?"

I hope such comments encourage discussion about the original agreement and perhaps launch a negotiation about a new and improved version with which all stakeholders feel comfortable.

### PeaceBuilders

Many schools are implementing a program called PeaceBuilders. PeaceBuilders is a research-driven, total climate change for schools, homes, workplaces, and communities—any place where people work, learn, play, or live. The program, available through Heartsprings Inc., in Tucson, Arizona, provides tools, ideas, and resources to reduce violence and aggression, and to enhance feelings of belonging and safety. The basic tenets of the PeaceBuilders program are *right wrongs, seek wise people, give up put-downs, praise people,* and *notice hurts.* Schools that have made a commitment and investment in the PeaceBuilders program have weekly assemblies in which students are honored, daily pledges to be PeaceBuilders, and classroom activities that teach the standards of the program.

RIGHT WRONGS.
SEEK WISE PEOPLE.
GIVE UP PUT-DOWNS.
PRAISE PEOPLE.
NOTICE HURTS.
   —PEACEBUILDERS

## Identifying the Problem, then Letting It Go?

We must help students acknowledge that everyone experiences daily conflicts. Conflict is a natural part of life. It is *not* a perfect world. Children often need help identifying a problem and the emotions that come with it. This step toward self-awareness is a key in building emotional maturity. Once we have named the problem and the emotion, then we can begin to decide how we are going to handle it. One very real option to explore is simply letting it go.

For some students (indeed, for many adults, as well), letting something go is a hard task. They are extremely sensitive or have a strong sense of fairness. It is next to impossible for them to let go of an issue. Other students seem to weigh the alternatives in their heads and decide that, in fact, this problem isn't worth getting worked up over, and it is best to let it go. In some situations, these children need to be encouraged to speak up because the problem is too serious to let go. They are sometimes seen as easygoing and unflappable, but may, in fact, be intimidated and fearful about confrontation.

Caplan (1997) notes how to determine if problems should be ignored or addressed: "Ignoring the problems is best when people put you down or tell you to do something that is against what you know is right (like if they tell you to try drugs or break school rules). In these cases, it's best to ignore." Following is a list of good guiding questions that students can ask themselves to determine whether or not a problem is worth letting go:

☆ Is anyone being physically hurt right now?

☆ Does the problem behavior have the potential to hurt someone?

☆ Is anyone's property getting or likely to get damaged?

☆ Was the conflict or behavior probably an accident?

☆ Could you simply point out the standard or agreement that has been broken?

☆ Can you use your own words, right now, to solve the problem?

☆ Is the problem one that you have had to deal with before?

☆ Has the person responsible already apologized?

☆ Are your feelings just hurt a little bit or are you really upset?

## Problem-Solving Agenda at Class Meetings

A variety of excellent conflict-resolution models are available to schools and classrooms. One aspect of most programs is class meetings, which are discussed earlier in this chapter. In many cases, you will facilitate the meetings. In intermediate classes, you may train students to facilitate. While the class meeting may have other agenda items, such as planning events, conducting business, planning fund-raisers, and discussing day-to-day issues, there may also be a regular problems-to-be-solved agenda item.

One successful technique for adding problems to the agenda is to post a clipboard or chart. During the week, as students have problems with other students or situations, they can put their names on the agenda with a key word to alert everyone to the nature of the problem. Ask students not to write the names of the students with whom they have conflicts, just a single word or short reminder phrase about the issue. Following is an example of such a chart:

## Problem-Solving Agenda
### February 13, 1998
1. Joe—blocks
2. Tara—lunch tables
3. Maria—broken pencils

When students write down a conflict, ask them to try to solve the problem first by letting it go, talking it out, or negotiating. If the problem is still not solved, then encourage the student to leave the item on the agenda for the next meeting. Occasionally, students will have problems that they don't want discussed in a meeting. In such cases, allow them to write *private* or simply *P* to alert you that they would prefer a private problem-solving opportunity at break or recess.

When the agenda item comes up in the meeting, ask each student whose name is on the list if there is still a problem. If you see one person's name up several times, encourage the student to summarize what some of the conflicts are or to address the one or two that are most important. The issues are often related, anyway. You might also use the strategy of taking up students' first issue and agreeing to come back to their additional agenda items after others have had a chance to share at least one.

In many cases, students have resolved the problem by the time the meeting is called. If such is the case, ask the student to put a line through his or her name. If the problem still needs to be solved, the student states the problem while everyone else listens attentively. If there are other students involved in the conflict, they may state their version of the conflict next. Ask the students involved if they have any suggestions for resolution. If resolution doesn't seem likely, then the facilitator asks others in the meeting to suggest possible solutions. The goal would be to arrive at a reasonable solution to which both parties agree. As the facilitator, restate the

WHEN STUDENTS WRITE DOWN A CONFLICT, ASK THEM TO TRY TO SOLVE THE PROBLEM FIRST BY LETTING IT GO, TALKING IT OUT, OR NEGOTIATING. IF THE PROBLEM IS STILL NOT SOLVED, THEN ENCOURAGE THE STUDENT TO LEAVE THE ITEM ON THE AGENDA FOR THE NEXT MEETING.

problem when necessary, encourage brevity, ask students to state their feelings, and acknowledge these feelings out loud. Be careful to allow others to contribute as needed, without letting it turn into a gang-up session. So often, the problem is resolved just by having it acknowledged in a public forum—by being heard.

Jeff Caplan (1998) emphasizes the class meeting strategy in his comprehensive program for schools and families. As students have more experience with this model, they begin to solve more of their own problems. Caplan admits that at first the facilitator must be vigilant in ensuring that the steps are followed. Eventually, with routine use, the pattern for solving problems becomes stored as a program in the brain. He also works with parents about using a similar format for family meetings. Caplan responds to questions teachers have had about the classroom meeting process.

1.  *What if one student has his or her name on the agenda fifteen times and dominates the meeting?*

    **Caplan:** When it comes time for problem solving, I say "Jeff, I see your name a number of times. We will solve your first problem and then go on to the next name on the list. We'll get to your second problem after other students on the agenda have solved their first problem." This approach helps Jeff prioritize the problems he puts on the list, beginning with those that are worth solving and what problems are worth letting go.

2.  *What if our class's agenda of student problems is three pages long and we can't get through it all in one meeting?*

    **Caplan:** Set a time limit for your meeting (twenty minutes in younger grades, thirty to forty minutes in older grades). Any problems that are not solved in one meeting come up first in the next meeting. In between meetings, students cool off and let some minor problems go. Remember, a three-page agenda has seventy-five indications that students demonstrated their skills for channeling their anger instead of fighting or tattling to the teacher! That's great!

3. *What if all the conflicts are with one person (who never puts any-thing down on the agenda!)?*

   **Caplan:** I let up to three people solve their conflicts with this one aggressive student. In other words, I have a rule that any student can receive a maximum of three feeling statements or solve three problems per meeting. On the second feeling, I ask that student, "Are you sure you can listen to another feeling?" If the response is yes, then we continue, but three is the limit so that the student doesn't melt down and get violent at recess afterward. I encourage students who still have conflicts to talk outside of meetings or to adopt solutions for other problems agreed to in class meeting.

On page 114 is a format that I have found helpful for all class meetings. You may copy it to use as is, or make changes you find appropriate.

## Mediating Problems and Students as Mediators

When students can't solve problems on their own or in a class meeting, you will probably have to mediate. I have seen some older children acquire the knack for mediation also, but more of-ten the responsibility will be yours. If you have an agreed-upon method for solving problems, then being the mediator is easy. If there isn't a plan, you will often be put in a position of having to be a judge. The whole dynamic of a problem-solving session be-comes two students competing with one another to have an adult judge them to be right in a conflict. It will become less of a win-win session. You will have to become a disciplinarian.

Agreeing upon a method for solving problems is an important step in resolving conflicts. A whole school may adopt a particular conflict-mediation and -resolution program, or individual teachers may wish to develop or adopt a method that works best within their classrooms. One excellent resource is Barbara Porro's *Talk It Out: Conflict Resolution in the Elementary Classroom.* Following is one such procedure that I developed that works quite well.

IF YOU HAVE AN AGREED-UPON METHOD FOR SOLVING PROBLEMS, THEN BEING THE MEDIATOR IS EASY. IF THERE ISN'T A PLAN, YOU WILL OFTEN BE PUT IN A POSITION OF HAVING TO BE A JUDGE.

# Generic Class Meeting Format

## Tools

+ agenda: for issues, problems, ideas, suggestions
+ talking stick: item passed around to people who wish to speak; only the person holding it is allowed to speak
+ problem-solving strategy: model for mediating problems to which all participants agree
+ decision-making model: method for consensus or voting to which all participants agree
+ clock or stopwatch for keeping time

## Ground Rules and Agreements

+ Listen actively; use talking stick when speaking.
+ Demonstrate respect for all members.
+ No put-downs; use compliments and praise.
+ Use the right to pass only occasionally.
+ Refrain from gossiping about agenda items after the meeting.

## Basic Meeting Format and Procedures

+ Sit in a circle, if possible; all must feel included and seen.
+ Briefly review agreements and procedures.
+ Agree about facilitator's role; is it okay for that person to speak without having the talking stick?
+ Choose timekeeper and set time limits.
+ Start with positive question or inclusion activity for all.
+ Allow time for compliments or praise.
+ Discuss feelings (see following example).

> A: "_____, are you ready to hear my feeling?"
> B: "Yes" or "No."
>    If "yes," then:
> A: "_____, I feel _____when you
>    _____."
> B: "_____, I understand you feel _____when I
>    _____."

+ Or send an urging message (see page 100).

> _____, I urge you to "stop touching my desk every time you go to the sink" or "keep sitting with me at lunch."

+ Address agenda items, including problems (prioritize if necessary and set time limits).
+ Close with a facilitator summary.

# Generic Problem-Solving Procedure for Mediator

Step 1: Students involved have taken time to cool off; they are not too upset or crying. They are ready to respond reflectively rather than reflexively.

Step 2: The involved students and you have agreed upon a time and place away from others, with minimal distractions.

Step 3: Check in with students to ensure that everyone agrees there is still a problem, and that together you all will attempt to find a solution acceptable to all.

Step 4: The first student describes the current problem and states her feelings about it. The second student summarizes and restates the first student's feelings. Remind students to keep statements brief, focused, and current, and help them identify their feelings.

Step 5: The second student describes the current problem from his point of view and states his feelings about the problem. The first student summarizes and restates. Again, prompt, restate, and summarize, as necessary.

Step 6: Briefly summarize and restate feelings of all people involved.

Step 7: Encourage each person to brainstorm possible solutions to this problem. Occasionally, someone will immediately have a short-term idea, then a long-term plan will develop later. Write all ideas down if you think it is necessary.

Step 8: All involved students agree to one or a combination of the possible solutions.

Step 9: Restate the agreement, writing it down if necessary, and get an oral commitment to the solution from all students. Ask them to shake hands, if they feel okay about that.

Step 10: Encourage students to apologize or find another way to make up any wrongdoing or show remorse. Students agree to let the problem go before they return to the class. Remind them that everything said in the meeting is confidential.

## The No-Blame Approach

Pat Belvel recently shared a model she uses that offers a way to solve students' problems without placing blame. This no-blame approach is based on the narrative model (also called the competency-based model) that Victoria Dickerson (1997) describes in *If Problems Talked.* The standard conflict-resolution model encourages students to state how another's behavior makes them feel. In a way, then, students don't take responsibility for their own feelings; rather they are placed in the situation of being the victim of another's actions. Their sad or mad feelings are caused by someone else: "I blame you for my feeling this way." In the no-blame approach "the problem is the problem." The model acknowledges that the problem certainly affects the child, parent, or teacher, but the focus is on identifying the problem or conflict, not on who did what to whom. As Belvel (1998) notes, "When no one is to blame and no one is labeled then everyone's task is to simply solve the problem and the problem becomes the enemy for everyone to rally around and defeat!" By focusing on the problem rather than seeking someone to blame, a student may avoid being labeled a trouble maker. When students are identified as the cause of problems, they are stuck with that label, and their good qualities are not always evident. By identifying the problem and not labeling the student, you create possibilities for actually solving the problem.

IN THE NO-BLAME APPROACH "THE PROBLEM IS THE PROBLEM."

## Handling Student Upsets

Even in the most brain-compatible classrooms, there will be student upsets and unexplained behaviors. When individuals feel threatened, confused, frustrated, excluded, or put down, they will react reflexively; most students' upsets are angry outbursts that are the result of unexpressed emotions. For such times, you need a handful of strategies ready that are not necessarily geared to solving problems. A variety of temporary techniques designed primarily to de-escalate emotional situations exist; select a technique from the following list to which you feel the individual student will respond best. If one doesn't work, try another quickly! Consideration of a child's developmental stage will likely help you select the appropriate response. Remember, however, that when reacting to emotions, humans are often soothed by actions that would seem appropriate only for young children: a cuddle, soothing words, a bandage!

### Touch

Consider immediately an appropriate hug or cuddle; placing your hand and arm around the student's shoulders, stroking her arm, drawing him close alongside your body, as if to protect him.

### Listen

Listen with full attention, focused eye contact, and a neutral or slightly empathetic facial expression. Give simple empathetic verbal responses such as "Oh" or "I see."

### Reflect Feelings

Acknowledge the student's feelings by naming the emotions: "You are really frustrated right now!" "I can hear that you are really angry at Maria!"

### Respond

There's nothing better than to have someone jump to your aid or assistance. With young children, you may need to stop the interaction or confrontation physically. When students are really upset, I use my secret weapon—an ice pack! Just about anything can be deescalated and comforted with a blue ice pack. Place it on a physical hurt, or use it to help students who are simply really upset "cool off"—literally. You can freeze clean, wet sponges in zippered plastic bags, too. Likewise, Band-Aids, a drink of water, a blanket, a comfy chair, or a lap can all help get the child through an emotional outburst.

While you are assisting students through upsets, resist the temptation to offer advice, deny their feelings, ask more questions, defend the other person, offer pity, say that you'll fix the problem, or give a philosophical response such as "Life is hard, isn't it?"

WHEN NO ONE IS TO BLAME AND NO ONE IS LABELED THEN EVERYONE'S TASK IS TO SIMPLY SOLVE THE PROBLEM AND THE PROBLEM BECOMES THE ENEMY FOR EVERYONE TO RALLY AROUND AND DEFEAT!
—PATRICIA BELVEL

Such responses only invalidate children's feelings and may inhibit their potential to solve the problem themselves. One of the most helpful books about this subject is Faber and Mazlish's (1980) *How to Talk so Kids Can Listen and Listen So Kids Can Talk.*

### *Problem-Solving Role Play*

As you begin to create and adopt a problem-solving model, make sure to have some students role-play the steps. Such role-play is a great opportunity for the actors in your class to show their improvisational skills. Ask several students to brainstorm situations that often happen in the classroom or out on the playground. A couple of students role-play possible problem-solving steps. Be sure to display the steps and refer to them as they come up in the role-play. Some students need this opportunity to see what problem solving looks like to feel that they can do it themselves.

## Interventions and Short-Term Discipline Plans

WHILE YOU ARE ASSISTING STUDENTS THROUGH UPSETS, RESIST THE TEMPTATION TO OFFER ADVICE, DENY THEIR FEELINGS, ASK MORE QUESTIONS, DEFEND THE OTHER PERSON, OFFER PITY, SAY THAT YOU'LL FIX THE PROBLEM, OR GIVE A PHILOSOPHICAL RESPONSE SUCH AS "LIFE IS HARD, ISN'T IT?"

Brain-compatible classrooms, although joyous and exciting places, may still have inappropriate student disruptions that demand intervention. Unacceptable behavior may require individualized discipline plans.

Take time to discuss with your students the differences between inappropriate and unacceptable behaviors. Inappropriate behaviors are the smaller acts that fall under the heading of inconsiderate. Put-downs, putting feet up on desk, and some of the other behaviors I've discussed would fall into this category. Unacceptable behaviors are any that physically, emotionally, verbally, psychologically violate the sense of security and safety in the classroom. Hitting, calling others derogatory names, and many deliberately unkind acts fall under this category.

You can usually use interventions to deal with inappropriate behavior. Interventions are really temporary redirection techniques. Use them to "turn inappropriate behavior into appropriate behavior temporarily with the least amount of attention, time, energy or disruption of class time" (Belvel 1995, 82). Choose from the list of strategies on page 120 to redirect inappropriate behavior:

If intervention doesn't work, that is, if you see a pattern of inappropriate behavior, you will need to solve the problem by discussing the behavior or giving consequences for it. Consequences for inappropriate behavior should be incremental and individualized, not one-size-fits-all.

When students do something that is unacceptable, you have only a few choices of what actions to take. Even in cases of unacceptable behavior, do your best to ensure that you are disciplining, not punishing students. Pat Belvel (1992) notes these differences between punishment and discipline. Punishment is really "control gained by enforcing obedience and order" (83). It is rarely related to the incident and is often threatening and demeaning. "Discipline connotes teaching, learning and instruction. It is training that corrects, molds, or perfects mental or moral character" (83). The delivery of discipline should be neutral, nonjudgmental, and full of positive alternatives.

The list on page 121 describes a few options you have for dealing with unacceptable behavior:

After trying many techniques in a learner-centered classroom, you may, as I did, find that you occasionally must create short-term discipline plans for individual students who have patterns of either inappropriate or unacceptable behavior. Be sure you have given them numerous opportunities to solve the problem on their own and have also taught them strategies they might use to solve them. Involve parents and the individual students in creating the plan. The plans should usually be short term and directed to very specific, repeated behaviors. Offer some modest, short-term incentives from which the student can select a few. For example, sometimes I note progress on a chart or send a note home to parents. Ensure that students know the consequences for not changing the behavior.

While we can never anticipate every problem or conflict that might arise in our classrooms, we can take a best guess and set up systems ahead of time that give us and our students patterns for solutions. With our students we will experience conflicts, but we can arrive at eventual resolutions by using the systems. We can then begin to count on the success we experience. We actually

WE ACTUALLY BEGIN TO UNDERSTAND THAT MOST PROBLEMS HAVE A REASONABLE SOLUTION AND THAT THERE REALLY CAN BE WIN-WIN SITUATIONS.

# Strategies to Redirect Inappropriate Behavior

**Body language**
Use eye contact, neutral facial expression, proximity to student.

**Time and silence**
Use "wait time" to alert students to the inappropriate behavior.

**Ignoring**
Selectively ignore behaviors intended to manipulate, engage, or resist.

**Broken record**
Keep repeating the expected appropriate behaviors.

**Move students**
Insist on students' sitting somewhere else to change behaviors.

**Class meeting agenda**
Redirect students to place their names on the problem-solving agenda.

Begin with the Brain, © 1999 Zephyr Press, Tucson, Arizona

# Options for Dealing with Unacceptable Behavior

## Consequences

agreed-upon logical consequences for unacceptable behaviors (not just inappropriate) such as loss of privileges, detention, cleaning up damage that was done, phone call to parents

## Time-out

agreed-upon time in a designated seat, another classroom, administrator's office

## Removal

as a last resort, to the office, counselor, by parent to the home begin to understand that most problems have a reasonable solution and that there really can be win-win situations.

## *Where to Begin*

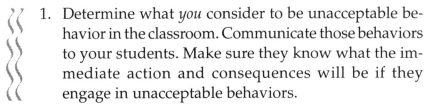

1. Determine what *you* consider to be unacceptable behavior in the classroom. Communicate those behaviors to your students. Make sure they know what the immediate action and consequences will be if they engage in unacceptable behaviors.

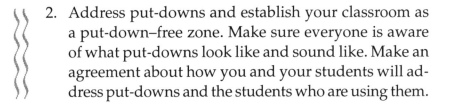

2. Address put-downs and establish your classroom as a put-down–free zone. Make sure everyone is aware of what put-downs look like and sound like. Make an agreement about how you and your students will address put-downs and the students who are using them.

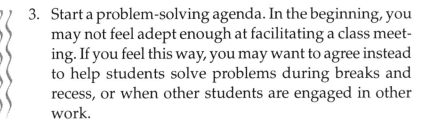

3. Start a problem-solving agenda. In the beginning, you may not feel adept enough at facilitating a class meeting. If you feel this way, you may want to agree instead to help students solve problems during breaks and recess, or when other students are engaged in other work.

# 8
# Shared Decision Making
*Creating Democratic Classrooms*

## Begin with the Brain

》 *Brain research over the last twenty-five years confirms that we construct our own understandings about the world around us through experiences, activities, and processes that have emotional and social elements.*

We are learning more every day from neuropsychological research regarding the importance of guiding children to develop social and emotional skills through firsthand experiences. To build a deep understanding of any subject, plant life cycles to technology, students must have opportunities to explore. It is through manipulation, experience, and process that the brain internalizes, makes connections, and remembers concepts. Democracy is one concept students must experience to be able to comprehend its meaning and be able to apply it to daily life.

## The Process Is the Point

Students' learning will not be powerful, nor will they be able to access it easily, if they experience the concepts and skills only in secondhand ways. Anytime someone or something other than the students themselves interpret new information, via lectures, demonstrations, pictures, videos, readings, the learning loses force. The least powerful learning takes place when the concepts are third-hand, that is, abstract or symbolic via notations, numerals, letters, words, icons.

IF WE ARE TRULY AT-TEMPTING TO CREATE LEARNER-CENTERED CLASSROOMS WE MUST CONSIDER DEVELOPING SYSTEMS THAT INCLUDE STUDENTS AS ACTIVE PARTICIPANTS.

Inviting students to be part of making even some of the decisions in the classroom may at first seem frightening to many educators. If we give children power, then who knows what they will or won't do. If we are truly attempting to create learner-centered classrooms, however, we must consider developing systems that include students as active participants. There is no question that the bulk of the curriculum may already be determined. There are also many schoolwide structures and systems that may be mandated and perhaps are nonnegotiable. But it is our job to orchestrate as many opportunities with which we feel comfortable for students to become problem solvers and decision makers.

In 1916, John Dewey published his classic *Democracy and Education.* In it he writes that, if we are to maintain our democratic society, we "must have a type of education which gives individuals a personal interest in social relationships and control, and the habits of mind which secure social change without introducing disorder" (115). If our nation is going to continue to maintain a democratic way of life, our students must have real-life experiences with democratic processes and the responsibilities that come with participatory governing systems.

Simply learning about democratic ideals through a textbook or even via a one-time mock election will not guarantee the deeper understandings that students will need to apply democratic principles as participating citizens in the real world. Michael Apple and James Beane (1995) describe two ways that schools can bring democracy to life: "One is to create democratic structures and processes by which life in the school is carried out. The other is to create a curriculum that will give young people democratic experiences" (9).

In what policies and decisions are you willing to have students participate? How can you create meaningful opportunities and allow students to generate their own ideas about developing events, planning activities, and setting policies?

# What Kinds of Decisions?

Your individual situation will dictate to what degree the students in your class will be able to make decisions and shape policy. In many schools the administration seems to mandate *all* policy, even that within individual classrooms, at least at first. Many teachers say that there are very few areas in which students might generate ideas and make decisions. Often, after a little investigating, you might find that you have more flexibility than you first thought. Your administration may be willing to consider well-thought-out ideas that students present in a professional, mature way. Besides determining which decisions your administration will or will not allow, you also need to reflect on the areas in which you are willing to give up some control and allow students to make decisions.

## Places to Start

Before you begin, you also have to decide which elements of the planning and decisions you will leave up to the students. You may want them to organize as much of an event as possible, including taking on all of the following responsibilities:

*getting administrative approval for the event*
*scheduling the event on the school's or classroom's master calendar*

SIMPLY LEARNING ABOUT DEMOCRATIC IDEALS THROUGH A TEXTBOOK OR EVEN VIA A ONE-TIME MOCK ELECTION WILL NOT GUARANTEE THE DEEPER UNDERSTANDINGS THAT STUDENTS WILL NEED TO APPLY DEMOCRATIC PRINCIPLES AS PARTICIPATING CITIZENS IN THE REAL WORLD.

*advertising and promoting the event*

*planning the details of implementation, such as getting a microphone and prizes, calling an assembly*

You also need to determine in what areas you will allow students to participate. The following descriptions are good places to start.

### Celebrations

During class meetings, encourage students to put on the agenda opportunities to plan parties, celebrations, and family gatherings. Often a group of students will suggest the class have a party on the day before a long school break. They form a planning committee and decide who will bring what for refreshments. With your approval they can plan games, costume contests, videos, and so on. I have always encouraged students to plan such parties well ahead of time, and if possible, to relate them to something we've been studying.

I often put family gatherings on the agenda for students to help plan. We usually organize these celebrations of learning as a culminating event for special units of study or when students have completed projects (see chapter 11 for more ideas). I try to have at least three or four such gatherings a year. Students have set up museums, art shows, performances, information booths, and interactive stations. We invite all family members and friends, as well as other members of the community who have some connection to what we have been studying. These gatherings are always wonderful community-building events.

### Schoolwide Events

Encourage students to brainstorm, plan, and organize some kind of activity suitable for whole school participation. Theme days, such as Backward Day, Crazy Day, or Spirit Day, are great ideas. You might also plan food drives, red ribbon weeks, and Earth Day celebrations. Planning these activities is especially helpful if there isn't an active student council to organize them.

## Community Service

Keep your eyes and ears open for ways to help out within your community. One winter, a local group requested donations for motel-size soaps and shampoos. They were donating them to homeless shelters and church groups that were making up toiletry bags for the needy. We saw the article in the local paper, and a group of students made up a flyer for the rest of the school. In a short time, we had collected a couple of boxes of supplies.

Looking for similar opportunities may fall on your own shoulders at first. You may want to take the initial initiative, then give over the planning to your students. As students and their families get the idea, soon other suggestions will come in as to ways the class can help. Early in the school year, for example, there is always a beach clean-up day. To be assigned to a local beach, I had to call and put our name on the list during the summer. Once school started, I announced to the class what part of the beach was ours. I said they could decline to participate or plan the rest of the activity on their own. They chose to plan it!

## Fund-Raising and Social Causes

Often students will decide to do some kind of activity to raise money for the class, for a local charity, or for a major social cause. Students in my class wanted to raise money for the class account, which went for field trips and other expenses or for whatever cause in which we were currently involved. They recognized the opportunity to have a bake sale every Wednesday at their lunch recess for the high school students at the adjoining campus. Different students helped each week. Often a parent helped supervise. Believe me, there's nothing like a hungry high school student to wipe out inventory!

During a unit on marine mammals, my students decided to raise money at the family gathering. Each research group had a booth and sold small items (magnets, jewelry, food) for less than a dollar. They wanted to send the money they raised to the charity that supported the animal they were studying: Save the Whales, Manatees, Dolphins.

## Handling Bigger Responsibilities

In a brain-based, learner-centered environment, our goal as educators is to facilitate opportunities for students to take on more responsibility in daily classroom decisions. The reality is that many students, especially older ones, are not able to handle the challenge immediately. In many cases, they have come to your class having had little success in previous classrooms. They may lack self-management and basic social skills. If others have always managed their behavior through rewards and punishments, they are often not capable of accepting the new, greater responsibilities we are asking them to take. As agents of change, we must carefully assist students to make the transition to responsible human beings.

When we teach children how to make good choices and give them opportunities to do so, we give their feelings of capability and self-esteem a boost. At school, just as at home, the shift from having adults making all the decisions to the children's beginning to make decisions for themselves should be gradual. It takes time. In addition, young children should be given opportunities to make only those choices that are appropriate to their developmental maturity.

James M. Harris (1989) discusses this complex issue. He states that there are two main rules parents and teachers must follow as they guide children toward making decisions and taking on responsibility:

☆ Children should not be allowed to make decisions in which irresponsible choices have potentially dangerous consequences to themselves or to others.

☆ Never allow children to make decisions that you can't live with. For instance, don't give students the impression that all decisions they make necessarily will be implemented and become part of policy if that simply isn't a distinct possibility.

Many teachers in schools and classrooms that have made the transition to more democratic procedures love to tell war stories of what the first year was like. When students are suddenly asked to be cooperative participants before they have mastered the basic social and emotional skills necessary, chaos can result. On the other hand, many students will immediately rise to the occasion. As Kohn (1996) notes, "Just as it takes the eyes a moment to adjust to the sunny outdoors after emerging from a dark room, so it takes the mind and heart a while to cope with freedom after having been expected to do what one is told" (96). Over time and with some success in making decisions about topics that don't have huge repercussions, students will acquire skills and their confidence will increase.

## Bigger Decisions

As students practice solving problems and making greater decisions you can increase their responsibilities. At various times I have placed students in charge of a variety of program choices, process decisions, and even curriculum selections:

☆ Organizing the schedule for the day or week, and figuring out how to work on the must-do activities while allowing time for may-do activities

☆ Setting deadlines for assignments and minimum requirements for projects and products

☆ Selecting and arranging themselves in work groups for special projects

☆ Creating selection criteria for their participation in certain activities

☆ Developing a rubric for assessment of their work

☆ Researching and investigating community resources for in-class presentations

☆ Designing systems for rotating use of special supplies or computers

☆ Determining content for parent communications or press releases

☆ Determining consequences for those who keep others from learning

☆ Suggesting content for the next unit of study

JUST AS IT TAKES THE EYES A MOMENT TO ADJUST TO THE SUNNY OUTDOORS AFTER EMERGING FROM A DARK ROOM, SO IT TAKES THE MIND AND HEART A WHILE TO COPE WITH FREEDOM AFTER HAVING BEEN EXPECTED TO DO WHAT ONE IS TOLD
— ALFIE KOHN

129

My caution about giving children responsibility for deciding the next unit of study is fairly straightforward. Students often request something that has been a hot topic on TV or in the movies recently. Whatever is big in the media will likely be something in which they insist they are interested: dinosaurs, black holes, asteroids, time travel, cloning, extraterrestrials. Many times these choices are not appropriate for in-depth units of study. They also leave you scrambling for resources and frustrated by the lack of opportunities for firsthand experiences.

Be cautious about turning over too much of the curriculum to student direction. Because we have so many standards to address and so much pressure to teach "the basics," I still prefer to select and orchestrate curriculum themes. Then, within the topic areas that I select, I encourage the students to develop areas of interest and related special projects. In this way, I refrain from directing all of the content and curriculum, but certainly I have ensured that I am addressing the curriculum requirements for that grade level.

I STILL PREFER TO SELECT AND ORCHESTRATE CURRICULUM THEMES. THEN, WITHIN THE TOPIC AREAS THAT I SELECT, I ENCOURAGE THE STUDENTS TO DEVELOP AREAS OF INTEREST AND RELATED SPECIAL PROJECTS.

## Decision-Making Possibilities

Many times, a simple majority vote taken by asking students to raise their hands seems like an absolutely perfect method for making decisions. It is efficient. In a heartbeat, you can determine whether or not a proposal has the support of the people. The problem with voting yea or nay is that there are inevitably winners and losers. If the decision is not one in which anyone has a lot at stake, then the losers will usually accept the decision peacefully and participate in the decided course. However, if the vote is close or if the stakes are high, be ready to deal with disgruntled losers.

Many new decision-making methods are being explored throughout workplaces, in schools, and even in governments. These methods are usually designed to gain consensus and promote various ways that participants can feel they have influenced the final decision in some way. Negotiations and compromise, when possible, become key factors in the process.

### Gradient System

I have often used this method for making decisions in my classrooms. Use a one-to-five gradient (or one to four) to allow participants to express their level of support for a given proposal (see the sample on page 132). When you present a proposal, everyone in the meeting states a number that corre-

sponds to the level of support they are willing to give to it. At Monarch Community School, the adult decision-making committees used an almost identical gradient to the one students eventually adopted.

Use a gradient when someone makes a proposal. If several ideas are being proposed, then the decision makers must consider each carefully to determine which one has the most support. First, ask a student to read the proposal aloud, then the facilitator restates it or writes it on the board. The process is similar to that for making a motion during a meeting. The facilitator asks if anyone needs any clarification in the language or other aspects of the proposal. Then the facilitator asks, "Are you ready to make a decision?" Students respond by using a "thumbs-up" sign, nodding their heads, or even quickly answering "yes." If someone isn't ready, then continue the discussion until everyone understands the proposal (see also Back-up Systems on page 137). Participants then show how much they are willing to support the project by stating a number from the gradient, either orally or by holding up the appropriate number of fingers. In a shared decision-making model, there is less of a need to have secret votes. The idea is for everyone to know how everyone feels about a given topic and for there to be no surprises.

## Determining Support

A strongly supported decision would be one for which most members cast a four or a five vote. Everyone loves the idea or at least really likes it. Even if a small percentage give it a three, it still has the potential of being strongly supported.

# Team Decision Gradient

5. Love the idea! Think it is the best solution. Will support it completely.

4. Like the idea. I'm supportive. Have positive feelings about most aspects.

3. Can live with the decision. Ambivalent about the results. Have no strong feelings for or against.

2. Do not really care for the idea. Not in strong opposition, but won't stand in the way.

1. Strongly oppose at this time. Will make attempts to stand in the way.

Begin with the Brain, © 1999 Zephyr Press, Tucson, Arizona

If a large percentage of the participants say that they can just "live with it," don't consider it a strongly supported decision. While technically it may have passed, it does not have the support of the people. Living with it does not mean that people will defend, support, work, volunteer, or aid in implementation. Such decisions are immediately evident in that many people vote two, a few vote three, and a very few vote one.

At Monarch, we agreed that, if someone gave a one to a proposal, we would not go forward until that person could be convinced to raise the level of support or until the proposal was revised. When someone gave a proposal a one or a two, then the facilitator would ask the question, "What would it take for you to give it a three?" Such a question gave the participant some responsibility to come up with a compromise and a solution, not just block the decision. Many times the compromise is in wording or a small detail that others overlooked. Once you revise, you start the entire voting process over. While this process may seem tedious at first, it gets easier as people practice it.

A three-point gradient may work better for younger students:

## Three-Point Gradient for Younger Students

3.  I really like this idea! I want to do it!

2.  I don't really care one way or the other. It doesn't matter to me right now.

1.  I really don't like this idea. I don't want to do it.

I have seen some large classes or groups use strategies to determine a mathematical average using the numbers. They determine a number below which the proposal does not pass. For instance, in a group of ten people, if four said they were a five, two said four, three said three, and one person said two, the average would be 3.9. In that group perhaps they said that the proposal needed to be at least a 3.5 to pass. It is a good idea to determine up front how much support you need for a given proposal. If the proposal is about major changes in policy or program, then it most likely demands a strong buy-in by all stakeholders; you certainly wouldn't want the consensus to be "We can live with it."

# A True Story

At Monarch Community School several years ago, the students organized and put on a marine mammal fair as a culminating activity on a unit of study. Each multiage group (kindergarten through fifth grade) had five to seven members. They were organized based on interest, and each group had to have a variety of ages and abilities. They all had to research their animal (gray whale, manatee, walrus, dolphin, sea otter, orca, sea lion, elephant seal) and put together an information booth for the evening fair. Each booth had to have brochures, fact sheets, a display board, artwork, and something to sell to raise money for the species. Students made small magnets, earrings, bookmarks, and badges. The most popular item was food. The gray whale group made soft pretzels in the shapes of plankton and shrimp, the gray whale's favorite food. The manatee group sold cups of "manna tea" (hibiscus herbal tea). The walrus group made clam chowder (clams are a staple of the walrus's diet). Each group sold items for no more than fifty cents.

The evening was a huge success. Many families and friends came to see the incredible displays the students had created. Some groups made more money than others, ranging from $22 to more than $60. As the groups looked at their individual efforts, they realized that the money combined would total more than $350. Some young voice in class spoke up and said that we should combine the money and give it to some local group. This brilliant student quoted me, saying, "Remember what Ms. K. says, we're supposed to think globally, act locally!" I could have hugged him! Many other students agreed that it was a good idea, but many felt that they had already made an oral commitment to the original charity and weren't sure it would be right to change. We needed to have a class meeting, discuss this possible change, and make a decision.

For the next intermediate class meeting, we put a proposal on the agenda: "All groups will contribute their booths' money to one classroom sum to donate to a local group." Students from the primary class who wished to participate were invited to join the meeting, too. The students brainstormed a couple of issues. Would it be fair to the people who had made purchases, thinking their money was going to one cause, to send it to another? To which local group would we contribute this *big* amount? Most students quickly noted that, as long as the money went to a cause associated with marine mammals, we didn't have to worry about misleading our patrons. Deciding which group to give the money to was more difficult. We live on Monterey Bay, and the number of ocean conservation groups in the area could wash you away. Someone finally suggested that we donate the money to our local (six blocks away!) UCSC Long Marine Laboratory. We had all visited the museum and touched tanks on numerous occasions, and we knew they were doing lots of research on sea lions, elephant seals, whale migration, and sea otters.

Even though everyone participating in the discussion seemed to think this proposal was a good one, we still needed to make a formal decision using our five point gradient model. We wrote the proposal on the board: "We agree to pool the money made at the marine mammal fair and give the whole amount to our local Long Marine Lab." We went around the group, asking for opinions from more than thirty students.

The response went something like 5, 4, 5, 5, 4, 4, 5, 5 . . . until we got to Chris. Chris said, "One." Our facilitator responded appropriately: "Please tell us, Chris, what it would take for you to vote three on this proposal?" Third-grader Chris replied that he had been reading the newspapers lately and knew that there were some controversial new buildings going up on the property near the lab. He didn't want our money to go to help fund the new buildings. When we asked him how we could change the proposal to ensure the money didn't go for the new buildings, he asked, "When you make the donation, can you ask them to use this money only for the museum and not for building any new buildings?" Others also felt this stipulation was a good one, and we added the statement to the original proposal.

Now as we went around the circle, the support was higher than ever, and when we got to Chris, he said, "Five!" Of course, he would; he had changed the whole idea! He had protected the endangered land and saved the class from having made a horrible charitable blunder!

As we neared the last of the group, we came to Steve, who said, "One." "What would it take to make it a three?" He replied, "I don't know; I don't have any more money to donate." When we explained that he didn't need to donate any money, we were using the money from the fair, he quickly changed his opinion to a five. Yeah! We achieved a consensus. Students held fists up into the air and shouted "Yes!!!" and a cheer erupted.

The two students who challenged the proposal are examples of participants you might find in adult groups. Chris didn't share pertinent information during the discussion. He often liked to create drama by waiting until the last minute to put a monkey wrench into the process, thus delaying the consensus. It seemed as though he timed his sharing of information to make himself look like a hero for knowing it, rather than sharing it during the discussion so the group could take it into consideration. I've seen many teachers on staff committees do the same thing.

Steve, on the other hand, is the group member who is present but whose mind wanders. He is somewhat apathetic, maybe because he doesn't really feel included. By asking him to explain his vote, we forced him to get clarification, thus empowering him as a part of the decision-making body. Questions such as the one we asked Steve work with adults who are not paying close attention, as well.

## Back-up Systems for Consensus

It is important to have strategies to fall back on should the consensus model get hung up in some way. If you have attempted to reach a consensus, and for some reason the decision continues to be weak (threes), or one or two individuals are blocking it, then have a default system for determining what to do. Many groups decide that if they spend a certain amount of time discussing and voting and cannot reach a consensus, then they will go with whatever proposal gets a simple two-thirds majority vote.

If time constraints demand you make an immediate decision, then you should also have an understanding about who will be responsible for making a decision for the group. If a class is getting used to making many of the decisions, they may not like it if you suddenly step in and take over. However, if you have discussed the possibility ahead of time and agreed that "teacher makes the decision if it needs to be made before our next class meeting," then everyone will be able to live with it.

## The Committee System
## for Classroom Management

Student committees can take over many little (and big) jobs as easily as can an overworked teacher. For many years I used committee systems in my classroom to facilitate students' involvement with organizational duties. I found this program to be popular in my classes, and students had heard about it before they even came into my class.

The success of this system is based largely on the students' daily experiences with group cooperation activities. The more they work together on related projects, the more the idea of taking over some housekeeping duties will seem natural, and students will eagerly complete such tasks.

Divide students into four groups on the first day of school, and assign each to one of four tasks (see lists below). During each of the three remaining quarters, redivide the students into four new groups and rotate the duties.

I had the committees meet once a week for thirty minutes, usually on Friday mornings just before our regular class meetings. They kept records of decisions they made and of individual students' assigned responsibilities. They shared this information during committee reports. They often met again during recess, at lunch, or occasionally after school to complete all of their tasks. They met with me when necessary.

### Maintenance Engineers

*Empty trash daily.*

*Clean sinks and counters.*

*Feed classroom pets.*

*Straighten the take-five corner.*

*Take the lunch count and attendance to the office.*

*Water plants.*

### Communications Specialists

*Answer intercom respectfully.*

*Answer the door.*

*Go to office and carry messages.*

*Pass out papers and other supplies.*

*Write and publish at least one issue of a class newsletter.*

*Write thank you notes to guests who have come to the class.*

### Special Events Coordinators

*Plan for guest speaker to come to class.*

*Assist with field trip preparations.*

*Plan a science experiment day.*

*Plan a theme day (for example, tourist, twin, backward).*

*Plan a cooking day.*

*Make arrangements for any special events being planned by the class, including fund-raisers.*

## Entertainment Planners

*Arrange for movies or videos that pertain to theme.*

*Nominate an AV monitor to set up equipment.*

*Tell class about upcoming TV shows that pertain to the theme.*

*Give periodic movie reviews.*

*Make up and perform a skit, puppet show, variety show for the class.*

## Kids' Social Action

I highly recommend books by Barbara A. Lewis. Her *The Kid's Guide to Social Action* has tons of ideas and suggestions about guiding children to become involved in community projects. The last third of the book is filled with resources: addresses, forms, survey templates, guidelines for press releases. These are wonderful springboards into taking action in your communities.

## Team Effectiveness

Take time to assess how well the democratic process is working with your students. At mid-year and again at the end, ask the students to respond in writing or discuss some of the following reflection questions:

1. Responsibilities were shared among the group's members.

2. Decision making was shared and promoted consensus.

3. The meetings were organized and we kept to an agenda.

4. As a group member I voiced my opinions on issues.

5. As a group member I accepted the different ideas of my teammates and attempted to work with them.

6. I willingly volunteered to accept responsibility for a class project.

7. As a team member I accepted decisions and helped support them.

## *Where to Begin*

1. At a class meeting or gathering, encourage the class to share in organizing a theme day. Use a simple majority vote to determine the theme. Help students brainstorm all the elements they need to plan the day successfully: location, participation, promotion, times, prizes, judging, rules. Help them form a committee or assign tasks. Start small at first! Make sure they choose something playful, but reasonable. You want them to experience success the first time. After the event, orchestrate a discussion to evaluate the day and determine whether it was a success. Use the information to plan an even more successful theme day.

2. Take time to teach a gradient decision-making process to your class. With the students, create a simple proposal about changing an everyday occurrence, such as the way they line up to come into class or the way they decide who gets to use the computers. Lead students through the gradient decision-making process, then ask them to abide by the decision for a trial period of one week. Encourage a discussion after the trial period to determine if they want to make any changes. While the first proposals shouldn't be too important, it is wise not to have meaningless exercises just to use the process.

# 9

# Student Choice in a Learner-Centered Classroom

*Orchestrating Opportunities*

## Begin with the Brain

*When we give students choices and opportunities to control the content and process of their learning, their motivation increases. When they are highly motivated with low stress, optimal learning can occur.*

When we see a choice, our brain chemistry changes (Ornstein 1991). Research indicates that, when learners look forward to doing an activity and feel as if they have some control over the type of task, they feel positive and motivated.

These feelings trigger the release of endorphins that promote a general sense of well being and confidence. Having choices allows the learner to feel more in control. Feeling in control of one's learning experience contributes to self-determination, self-confidence, and empowerment.

# The Choice Challenge

One of the more challenging offerings classroom teachers can give students on a regular basis is the opportunity to choose. As we attempt to educate our students in traditional school settings, the task of giving students choices in what they can learn, how they will learn it, how they will demonstrate their understanding, and how to express themselves seems overwhelming. The job would not seem quite as difficult if we were sure that the students already knew how to make appropriate choices. But we fear that if we give students freedom to make their own decisions regarding learning, they will abuse the privilege and make poor choices or actually choose not to learn!

To alleviate our fears, we can begin to learn how the brain makes choices. There are many strategies for structuring and limiting selections so students can make good choices. We must understand the following:

☆ how the brain detects a pattern, selects a program, and makes choices

☆ how to guide children in making appropriate choices

☆ how to structure curriculum choices to allow for a wide range of student abilities, learning styles, and intelligences

☆ how to limit choices to help children select processes

☆ how to provide choices that build children's self-esteem

# How the Brain Makes Choices

As I note in chapter 3, Leslie Hart (1998) describes the brain's process for making decisions, going into action, and ultimately, learning. Learners must first evaluate the situation, task, or need (observe, detect, and identify the pattern or patterns); otherwise they simply do not know what the problem or task is. When given choices and situations in which they have no prior experience, relevance, context, or personal meaning, learners do not observe a connection and therefore don't even recognize any viable choices. In other words, they won't implement programs for which there is no frame of reference. Many times I have heard teachers lament the fact that students never choose a particular station or center. After some reflection, we often determined that the students didn't really understand what the activity was or its purpose; while it may have made sense to the teacher, it didn't have a meaningful context for the learner.

LEARNERS MUST FIRST EVALUATE THE SITUATION, TASK, OR NEED (OBSERVE, DETECT, AND IDENTIFY THE PATTERN OR PATTERNS); OTHERWISE THEY SIMPLY DO NOT KNOW WHAT THE PROBLEM OR TASK IS.

Another problem arises if we always direct students; we have no way of knowing if they are able to detect patterns, select programs, and implement them. As students have opportunities to evaluate, select, and implement their own choices that reflect their own personal connection, they will become more confident with making choices. If students have been overdirected, they may mistrust their own abilities for evaluating situations and making selections. Hart (1998) defines the first step of learning this ability as "the extraction, from confusion, of meaningful patterns"; the second step is "the acquisition of useful programs" with which to implement the learning (132).

Humans repeat what Hart calls the pattern-program cycle of learning thousands of times a day. The brain receives input through all the senses, matching the external clues and cues to its stored memories and patterns and making its best guess as to the most effective program to implement. When a stored program doesn't work in the new situation, creativity comes into play, and through trial and error, we construct new programs to store.

Simply stated, students must *detect, select, try,* and *modify* when making and implementing choices. Following is a description of each of these steps.

**Detect**   Identify a pattern, a problem, an option.

**Select**   Analyze possibilities, determine a strategy, and make a commitment.

**Try**   Go into action, implement a strategy, make an attempt.

**Modify**   Creatively adapt strategies to fit new situations; adjust and combine known patterns of action to construct a new program.

## Discovery Play

Not all choices and experiences in the classroom must have immediately discernible patterns or be based on every student's prior experiences. Indeed, especially in primary classrooms, many choices and centers will simply have objects that invite discovery play. Interesting games, manipulatives, toys, and real-world objects will get children's attention and may or may not have a specific learning objective or product attached. The entire point of the choice is for students to have an opportunity to experience the objects and start to recognize patterns associated with that experience.

Students can engage in discovery play alone or with others, without any prompts or with a facilitator's encouragement and inquiries. It is through these free exploration periods that students learn to construct their own knowledge based on previous experiences.

Brooks and Brooks (1993) note that constructivism occurs when children are allowed the freedom to explore, inquire, construct relationships, and search for their own understandings rather than follow other people's logic.

Mary Baratta-Lorton (1976) and her husband began the Math Their Way program nearly twenty-five years ago. They have always insisted that children need to have ample time to freely explore learning materials that they may use later to help them understand skills and concepts: "Without free exploration children's play interests are unsatisfied, and until this need is fulfilled, the children will pursue this priority relentlessly" (2). But of course, there must be some guidelines for presenting choices so that students don't feel overwhelmed.

## Limiting Choices

Opinion varies greatly regarding how much personal choice students should have when it comes to learning. With our focus on standards and state-mandated curricula, we have less flexibility in allowing students to determine what they learn. However, we should still offer students many opportunities to choose how they learn skills and concepts, and a variety of ways to demonstrate their understanding for assessment. I have seen two extremes, neither of which is effective:

- ☆ Classrooms offer no choices; all students do every activity directed by the teacher.
- ☆ So-called "free" or "alternative" classrooms in which there are an overwhelming number of learning centers or activity areas around the room; children are encouraged to "Go, be free, and learn"; there are no requirements.

You need to develop a balanced program of musts and mays. You will have activities, processes, tasks, and experiences that you want *all* your students to participate in and complete. Perhaps you want all students to experience the same process so that students have a common understanding when you give them extension activities. You will also sometimes want all students to complete a similar task and have a finished product.

I often gave all students in my class a book-writing project, self-portrait, multimedia project, math game, novel contract, or research report that they had to complete by a certain deadline. I expected all students to meet the same basic guidelines for each project. I didn't give them much choice about the activity itself, but they did choose the specific content within the project or report. These musts often served as benchmarks or portfolio pieces for assessment. Because the standards were the same for all, we developed a common rubric to evaluate them.

SINCE MANY CHILDREN HAVE NO PRACTICE AT MAKING CHOICES, INTRODUCE THEM TO THE PROCESS GRADUALLY.

Mays could be several different types of extension or enrichment activities related to the unit or a lesson. While the tasks should be somewhat equal in scope, and time and effort needed, they may be more open ended to encourage students to elaborate and create unique responses.

### Beginning Choice

Not only are many children's school experiences directed, their home life and after school time is often scheduled and planned, as well. This problem crosses socioeconomic boundaries. Children in affluent families are often shuttled from activity to activity, with weekends filled with performances, sports, and community activities. Children in impoverished communities are often housebound after school or in organized daycare programs. Neighborhoods are sometimes so unsafe that children are allowed only to stay inside and watch TV. There aren't many choices that offer children practice. Since many children have no practice at making choices, introduce them to the process gradually.

In the beginning, give students only a few choices. Young children may not be developmentally ready for more than a few options. Even older students who have been in tightly organized and directed classrooms may be overwhelmed with too many choices at first. To start, include activities that offer the same degree of difficulty. Remember, though, to include activities that address a variety of learning styles and intelligences. Structure them in such a way as to allow for a wide range of abilities. Some teachers begin introducing choice through homework assignments.

Three examples of choices in assignments are on pages 148, 149, and 150. The first is for a thematic unit on flight and the Wright brothers in an intermediate class. The second is the culminating assignment for O'Dell's *Island of the Blue Dolphins*. The examples clearly include opportunities for students to express themselves artistically, dramatically, musically, and verbally. There is also one opportunity to work with a partner. Students can earn the same number of points for all assignments. The expectations about what should be included are clearly stated. There is no obvious benefit to choosing one over another. Students may comment on the fact that one appears easier than others, but you can use this statement to lead into a discussion about multiple intelligences.

Several experiences with these kinds of choices will give the students a sense of trust, security, and consistency—all brain-compatible elements! Another benefit is, after seeing some of the products that the other students come up with, they will be more willing to try activities that challenge them. Soon you might expand the list, varying the ability levels and perhaps giving more points or a higher grade to some. Some of the choices might be open ended, with less structure and more room for creativity and student inspiration. Such opportunities require students to evaluate more to make decisions and choices; they must choose based on their strengths, their ability, and the grade they want, as well as on other criteria.

Remember that a student will rarely choose something with which her brain does not have experience unless she has acquired enough confidence in her abilities over time to risk choosing a variety of tasks. For example, if you include creating a diorama of a scene from a book as a choice, but you have not discussed what dioramas are or constructed them in other contexts, you run the risk

REMEMBER THAT A STUDENT WILL RARELY CHOOSE SOMETHING WITH WHICH HER BRAIN DOES NOT HAVE EXPERIENCE UNLESS SHE HAS ACQUIRED ENOUGH CONFIDENCE IN HER ABILITIES OVER TIME TO RISK CHOOSING A VARIETY OF TASKS.

147

# Homework Assignment on the Wright Brothers
From Monarch Community School

Choose one of the following. Each is worth up to 10 points. You may work with a partner only on item 3.

1.  **Draw** a picture of the Wright brothers' airplane, the *Wright Flyer*. Use 12-by-18-inch white paper; color the picture. Include all major details of the design.

2.  **Dramatize** in a one- to two-minute skit for the class what Orville might have said or thought during the historic twelve-second flight and immediately afterward.

3.  **Compose** a poem or lyrics to a song that commemorates the historic flight. Include references to the plane, the people, the location, and the flight itself.

# Culminating Assignment for Scott O'Dell's *Island of the Blue Dolphins*
### From Monarch Community School

After reading the novel, follow the instructions below. Be sure to do your *personal best*. Use *lined* paper for *writing* and *unlined* paper for *drawing*. *Put your name and the date at the top of each page*. List the number of each item you respond to. Put all your hard work together in a *decorated folder*.

**Complete at least six (6) of the following items.**

1. **Compare** the villagers (Karana's people) to the Aleuts. Note at least five ways that they are alike and different.

2. Skim chapters 3 and 4. **Describe** in a short paragraph what happened when the Aleuts tried to cheat the villagers.

3. Skim chapter 6. In a short paragraph or in a detailed drawing, **describe or illustrate** what the villagers had done to prepare for the Aleuts' return.

4. **Draw** a picture of the things Karan packed to take with her on the trip.

5. **Describe** the events that took place when Karana had to go back for Ramo. Or **draw** at least three scenes that show what happened.

6. **Imagine** that you are Karana. **List** the fears you would have if you were left on the island. **Tell** some ways that you could overcome your fears.

7. **Describe** why it is hard for Karana to make weapons. **Judge** why you think she made the decision.

8. In chapter 10, Karana makes a decision to turn back the canoe. **Tell** what decision you would have made and why.

9. Skim chapter 12. **Draw** a detailed picture of Karana's new house as it is described.

10. **List** as many items as you can that Karana had to make while alone on the island. **Evaluate** the items to decide if it was a necessity or a luxury. Next to each, **note** which you think it is.

11. **Desribe** and **list** all the animals Karana had as friends or "family." **Rate** them according to which you like best. **Organize** the list, putting the ones you like best at the beginning.

12. Karana demonstrated many traits: creativity, caring, perseverance, common sense, responsibility. **Choose** one of these traits and **tell** about instances from the story in which Karana shows this trait.

13. **Draw** a headstone for Rontu's grave. **Write** an appropriate epitaph for it.

14. **Describe** in a short paragraph or **draw** pictures of the types of foods Karana eats.

15. **Describe** some of the natural disasters that occur in chapter 27. Or **draw** a picture of what Karana might have seen.

16. **Describe** in a short paragraph what you think Karana's thoughts and feelings are as she leaves the island.

# Book Projects
From Monarch Community School

## Choose One

1. Imagine you are a Hollywood screenwriter. In a one-page writing, describe what story scenes you would film and what scenes you would not film and why.

2. Draw a comic strip of the plot.

3. Create a board game of the plot. Tell how the game relates to the story.

4. Write a one-act play about one important chapter in the book.

5. Select a key scene from the story and create a diorama of it.

6. Draw the main characters on large paper. Include collage pictures and words from magazines to describe the character.

7. Create a crossword puzzle of the characters and main elements of the story.

8. Write a one-page new ending for the story.

9. Perform a puppet or finger puppet show about one aspect of the story.

10. Write a newspaper-style article as if the story were happening today.

11. Create a mobile of the story. Parts of the mobile will represent various characters or scenes.

12. Develop a filmstrip or create overhead transparencies to tell the story.

13. Create a new design for a book cover. Use the inside flap to write a short summary of the story.

14. Write the essence of the story in a poem.

15. Pantomime the story line for the class.

16. Propose a possible video game that uses the story elements.

17. Paint or sketch at least three key scenes from the story.

18. Compose a rap or song (it's okay to use a common melody) that tells the story.

19. Perform a monologue for the class of something the main character may have been thinking or pondering at some point during the story.

that students won't have any experience or a context for dioramas; their brains won't interpret and recognize it as a true choice. At first, make sure that the selections on a list or in centers are similar to those you have done in class before. Once students have a pattern of making successful choices, they might be comfortable taking a risk on a choice with which they are not familiar, choosing to find out what it is and making it.

## Primary Choice Centers

In primary classrooms that are already designed around centers, teachers are usually able to create systems for some choices. Even in classrooms where three groups of students are simply doing three different activities, you can work in a way to allow for some "mays."

### *Choice Boards*

Schedule students for three or four center rotations, then allow them to choose their last one. Display the assignments for centers on a board with labeled clothespins, tongue depressors, or 3-by-5-inch cards in pockets. As students arrive in the morning, they check the center board, determine where they will begin that day, and select something they may do. They take their name stick or

card and place it at the sign for the center they would like as their free choice. Limit the number of students in each choice center; the first four, for example, get to be in that center. If you have students who are chronically late, they may be motivated to get to class early or on time because that may be the only way to get into the centers they want. If tardiness is *not* their fault, be sure to let them occasionally choose on the day before.

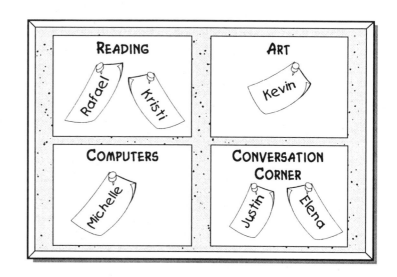

### *Passports or Center Schedules*

To facilitate the rotations for a whole week, some teachers fill out schedules for Monday morning. Students keep them in their learning logs, in a pocket folder, or in their supply bins as they travel to the different activities. Examples of these items are on pages 153 and 154.

### *Free Choice Time*

Many teachers have discovered that it can be difficult, especially in primary classes, to have some children doing "musts" and others doing "mays" at the same time. What seems to work better is to have students do their required rotation first, then have specific times for free choice. Some students actually go back to centers where they needed to complete some work. Others, like my youngest son, love this time of the day because they get to do what they want without worrying about completing anything! Of course, you need to have a system in place that ensures fair time at all the centers. Often the fastest, most aggressive students get to the blocks first, or some students take over the computer stations every day. We had a rule that a certain group of students had first choice on certain days.

Some centers are always in your classroom: computers, art, drawing, listening. You can also create seasonal or special-project centers. I rotate certain materials every couple of weeks. I put Legos away for a month or so; when I brought them back out, they were a hit all over again. You can put away puzzles, games, manipulatives, dress-up trunks, even certain books for a while, then reintroduce them. By rotating items, you keep children from doing the same things every day and encourage them to try new things.

### *The High Scope Program Alternative*

The High Scope Program for early childhood education takes a more radical approach to choice in the primary grades: they have actually built the whole program based on the idea that children can and should be able to choose what they are going to work on

# Weekly Schedule from Monarch Community School

Name _____

Group _____  Week of _____

| Monday | Tuesday | Wednesday | Thursday | Friday |
|--------|---------|-----------|----------|--------|
| Center 1 ___ | Center 1 ___ | Center 1 ___ | Center 1 ___ | Center 1 ___ |
| Center 2 ___ | Center 2 ___ | Center 2 ___ | Center 2 ___ | Center 2 ___ |
| Center 3 ___ | Center 3 ___ | Center 3 ___ | Center 3 ___ | Center 3 ___ |
| Center 4 ___ | Center 4 ___ | Center 4 ___ | Center 4 ___ | Center 4 ___ |
| Center 5 ___ | Center 5 ___ | Center 5 ___ | Center 5 ___ | Center 5 ___ |

# Rotation Schedule from Monarch Community School

| Sea 1 | Earth 1 | Sky 1 |
|---|---|---|
| Student | Student | Student |
| Student | Student | Student |
| Student | Student | Student |
| Student | Student | Student |

| Sea 2 | Earth 2 | Sky 2 |
|---|---|---|
| Student | Student | Student |
| Student | Student | Student |
| Student | Student | Student |
| Student | Student | Student |

| Monday | Computers | Spelling and Vocabulary | Choice Centers | Spelling and Vocabulary | Meet with Ms. K |
|---|---|---|---|---|---|
| 11:10-11:35 | Sea 2 | Earth 2 | Sea 1 | Earth 1 | Sky 1 and 2 |
| 11:35-12:00 | Earth 2 | Sky 2 | Earth 1 | Sky 1 | Sea 1 and 2 |
| 12:00-12:25 | Sky 2 | Sea 2 | Sky 1 | Sea 1 | Earth 1 and 2 |

| Monday | Computers | Spelling and Vocabulary | Choice Centers | Spelling and Vocabulary | Meet with Ms. K |
|---|---|---|---|---|---|
| 11:10-11:35 | Earth 1 | Sky 1 | Earth 2 | Sky 2 | Sea 1 and 2 |
| 11:35-12:00 | Sea 1 | Earth 1 | Sea 2 | Earth 2 | Sky 1 and 2 |
| 12:00-12:25 | Sky 1 | Sea 1 | Sky 2 | Sea 2 | Earth 1 and 2 |

each day. Students meet in small groups with an adult facilitator to discuss what they want to work on. They make a commitment, then have a work time at the appropriate center that can last up to an hour. The centers might have art materials or manipulatives that students can explore freely, or several may have activities based on a class unit. When the work time is up, students return to their groups; individually, they tell what they learned during their work time.

Managing this program can be quite a complex task. Teachers continue to move around the centers to prompt, ask questions, encourage, and help children process what they are doing. In some cases, teachers are actually noting students' participation and progress on a record sheet. The teachers are constantly looking for the teachable moment. At other times during the day, they might do a lesson based on what insights a few children discovered in a center.

## Guiding Students' Choices

As I mentioned earlier, one reason teachers are often wary of giving students opportunities to choose what they learn and how they learn it is that we know there are those who don't seem to rise to the challenge and ultimately make poor choices. We know that, although they appear to be trying, many students have a difficult time consistently making good choices. Following is a list of some common complaints teachers have:

- ☆ Students always choose the same center or activity, perhaps even dominate there.
- ☆ Students seem always to choose activities that don't challenge them.
- ☆ Students don't really choose anything; they wander around and often disrupt others.
- ☆ Students seem to choose only "fun" activities, such as art, drama, or play, and avoid anything that involves writing, reading, or projects.

Before I talk about how to take action and when it's necessary to do so, I want to caution you about assuming the student is being lazy or choosing activities that don't challenge. Students need times in their day during which they can experience self-determination and build self-confidence. Their choices will be based on their own needs, desires, and preferences. Some will need to do the same activity over and over to build self-esteem and feel empowered doing something at which they are successful. By letting children do the same thing over and over, you allow them to become an expert at that task. We all have such tasks we enjoy and work on because we're good at them: hobbies, crossword puzzles, golf, quilting, running. We never become bored with them.

You should, however, take action in a couple of situations. If a child is dominating a center and other students are not getting to participate fully, then guide that student to allow the others to participate. If that doesn't work, guide him to make other choices. I always try to determine if the other students truly need the student to move on rather than rely solely on my own observations. Many students love having the expert at their center; it puts them in good company: "We like it when Matt is here; he always comes up with great ideas for the blocks!" or "When Kurt is with us at the computer station, we know we have someone to help us if we need it." It also builds students' self-esteem to allow them to help other students, which is always a good characteristic for your students to develop.

If I decide I need to do something, I tell the student that she has had a lot of time at the center. I honor how successful she has been and how good she is at the task; then I insist she choose from one of the other centers for the next few days. You can negotiate or bargain with the student, but make sure she understands that the other students need her to move on for a while.

When students are choosing activities from a list, such as the inquiry lists on pages 158, 159, and 160, they often repeatedly select only those they think are "easiest." Use the list as an opportunity to discuss the probability that the task requires them to use a strong intelligence. I was the kind of student who *always* chose tasks that involved performing and presenting. Being a strong interpersonal and bodily-kinesthetic learner, these types of tasks always seemed easiest to me. I would keep choosing them until someone demanded, encouraged, asked, prompted, requested that I try something else. From those personal experiences, I know that students develop a variety of skills if you occasionally require them to choose a task that requires them to use one of their weaker intelligences.

If I have a student who needs a nudge to try something new, I often just cross out a few of the choices on the list and discuss with the student why I'm doing so. Avoid making the request sound punitive. I always let students know how successful they have been with the choices they have been making. I also reassure them that I want them to be the best, well-rounded learners they can be. Students and I will often set goals for how long or how many times the choices will be limited before they can go back to have truly free choice again.

Some students seem to avoid choices that involve certain tasks or skills, such as writing or reading. Students may also avoid activities that require them to interact with other students or expect them to draw or use their bodies. I have often used systems that require students to choose from various categories of activities. It looks kind of like ordering from a Chinese restaurant: one from column A, one from column B. I group writing choices on one list, art choices on another, and performances on yet another. I then require students to choose one item from each list. See, for example, *The Wind in the Willows* assignment on page 160.

## Coping with Decision-Making Difficulty

Some students will have difficulty making choices or sticking with their decisions because they have too much input or too many possibilities. Often they have not had experience with making successful decisions. If students seem to lack confidence in making choices, meet with them briefly after they make choices. Give them feedback and reassurance about the selection. A smile, a comment such as "That activity seems like it will be so much fun for you!" or a thumbs up may be all they need to feel acknowledged and confident.

# Keepers of Our Earth: "In the Pond"

From Monarch Community School

Inquiry Projects: "Mays"
Due Monday, March 11

In addition to *writing the essay* "What I Learned" and *answering the key questions*, choose the appropriate number of *inquiry projects* from the list below. Choose carefully and do your *personal best*.

Sea and Sky groups choose *one* project; Earth group, choose at least *two*.

1.  **Create** a colorful poster that illustrates the life cycle of a frog.

2.  **Create** a mobile that illustrates a food chain that might be found in a pond.

3.  **Carve** or **sculpt** a pond animal out of wood or clay; share it with the class. Be prepared to tell something about the animal.

4.  **Make something** useful out of tules that would help in the daily life of the Ohlones.

5.  **Write, define,** and **illustrate** at least ten pond and herpetology words for a children's dictionary. Use good paper and colored pencils or crayons. Spiral bind the book, or make copies, if you choose.

6.  **Interview** a naturalist, water biologist, herpetologist, or park ranger. **List** at least ten questions and their answers.

7.  **Compose** and **perform** a song about ponds or things you learned during our unit. You can make up words to a familiar tune, if you prefer.

8.  **Memorize** and **perform** for the class a pond play or puppet show. Ms. K has two from which to choose, or you can write your own. You may work with one or two other people on this one.

9.  **Draw** at least four scenes from our literature selection, Kenneth Grahame's *The Wind in the Willows*. Include scenes that are about river or canals. Bind your illustrations into little books, if you wish.

10. **Research** blue-green algae as a food source for humans. Present your findings to the class. Bring in a recipe using algae or some to sample.

If you have an idea of your own, submit your proposal!

# Keepers of Our Earth: "Down on the Farm"

From Monarch Community School

Inquiry Projects: "Mays"
Due Monday, April 11

In addition to *writing the essay* "What I Learned" and *answering the key questions*, choose the appropriate number of *inquiry projects* form the list below. Choose carefully and do your *personal best*.

Sea and Earth groups choose at least *one* project; Sky group, choose at least *two*.

1. **Create a display** of pictures and examples of various ways in which we use corn. Cut pictures from magazines or draw your own. **Categorize** and **label** the examples.

2. **Create a display** of early farm tools and simple machines. Cut out pictures from magazines or draw them on your own. **Label** them and include brief **descriptions.** Hint: Look in *Farmer Boy* or the *Farm Book.*

3. **Create an illustrated time line** of agricultural developments. Use a long sheet of 18-inch-wide butcher paper, or do a miniature version on cash register tape. Include years in which the various machines were invented and crops were introduced.

4. **Prepare a demonstration** on food preservation techniques. Include ways early farmers and early American Indians preserved food as well as contemporary techniques. Do your demonstration for the class.

5. **Write, define, and illustrate** at least ten farm words for a children's dictionary. Use good paper and colored pencils or crayons. Spiral bind the book, or make copies, if you choose.

6. **Create a three-dimensional display** of a farming scene. It can be about early farmers or an ancient civilization. Make sure the base does not exceed 2 feet by 2 feet. Use clay, papier-mâché, pipe cleaners, and other items. Label the various elements.

7. **Interview** a farmer. List at least ten questions and the farmer's answers.

8. **Prepare a small cookbook** of at least eight recipes for apples or corn. Design a cover and illustrate some of the recipes. Try one at home!

9. **Compose and perform a song** about farming or things you learned during our unit. You can make up words to a familiar tune, if you prefer.

10. **Memorize and recite** for the class the poem "The Ballad of Johnny Appleseed." Use gestures, a costume, puppets, or rhythms.

If you have an idea of your own, submit your proposal!

# *The Wind in the Willows* **Book Project**

From Monarch Community School

**Due Thursday, March 21**

After reading *The Wind in the Willows,* select and complete the appropriate number of projects from the following list. Do your *personal best.* Assemble written inquiries in a decorated cover. Spelling, sentence structure, and comprehension are important! Copy written inquiries to improve neatness and correct mistakes. You may check out copies of the book.

Earth group: Choose a minimum of *two* projects; *one must be written.*

Sky group: Choose a minimum of *three* projects; *one must be written.*

Sea group: Choose a minimum of *four* projects; *two must be written.*

1. **Describe** in a well-written paragraph how Mole meets Ratty at the beginning of the story.

2. **List** the four main characters and write a couple of sentences that describe each one and tell who they are.

3. **Sequence** on a time line at least six things that happen to Toad from his prison escape to his arrival at Ratty's home. Be creative! Use symbols and decorate with pictures.

4. **Draw** each of the four main characters using information in the book.

5. **Describe** in a well-written paragraph the hobbies or fads to which Toad is attracted.

6. **Dramatize** for the class Toad's monologue on page 192 ("Ho, ho, what a clever toad I am!")

7. **Recite** Toad's song from pages 192–193 for the class.

8. **Create** a storyboard (separate scenes, as in a comic book) of the series of events that take place in chapter 5, "Dulce Domum." Write a brief description under each scene.

9. **Create** small clay figures of at least two main characters.

10. **Design** a diorama or triorama of one of the following scenes:

    Recovering Toad Hall from the Wild Wooders

    The bargewoman and Toad on the canal

    Toad's escape from prison

    Ratty and Mole's picnic in chapter 1; don't forget to include the otter!

11. **Describe** in two well-written paragraphs Toad's clever escapes from Toad Hall and prison.

12. **Paint** a scene from the story using watercolors. Write a brief description at the bottom.

13. **Evaluate** whether Toad is a likable character. In a well-written paragraph, describe some of his faults and gifts, then give your final decision.

Make up an inquiry of your own and submit it for approval!

Sometimes students will jump from center to center; they can't seem to stay at one. They may have hyperactive or other attentional disorders; some students seem to have difficulty sustaining attention for more than about eleven minutes (I've noticed that this is about the same amount of time between commercials during TV shows!). But many students are just curious about what others are doing or need a break every few minutes. I always encourage these students to go scout what others are doing, get a drink, walk around (a little), then return to the area they have chosen.

When I was in school and was given a chance to choose a project, I always wanted to find out what my friends were doing first. I would be a social butterfly, going around asking the other students what their choices were before I could make my decision. In some cases, I took up most of my work time! If my teacher had said, "Okay, Martha, you have five minutes to discuss with a friend what your choice will be," I know I would have hustled and decided quickly.

## Goal Setting

Students must begin to develop internal motivation for doing tasks and activities; developing this skill will help them make better decisions about their personal goals, as well as school goals. As Pierce Howard (1994) notes, "Internal motivators are developed by participation in goal setting and problem solving, as opposed to allowing others to set your goals, make your decisions, and solve your problems" (192). If students don't know their own goals and don't have a clue about how activities relate to them, they may not be able to engage. You might include some activities in goal setting for teams. I also have older students write down their daily goals in their journals after they have recorded the daily agenda.

### *Homework Choices*

An excellent way to incorporate choices into students' daily learning is to have self-directed homework assignments, such as the one on page 163. Susie Phanton, a multiage primary teacher in Santa

INTERNAL MOTIVATORS ARE DEVELOPED BY PARTICIPATION IN GOAL SETTING AND PROBLEM SOLVING, AS OPPOSED TO ALLOWING OTHERS TO SET YOUR GOALS, MAKE YOUR DECISIONS, AND SOLVE YOUR PROBLEMS.
—PIERCE HOWARD

Cruz, California, created these homework choices. Prepare a list of possibilities each week from which students can select activities to do at home (see example on page 164). Make sure parents understand that their children are supposed to choose from the list. Explain this policy at a back-to-school night or in a brief note home.

Some students may need suggestions for what to do each day, not just "By the end of the week, complete four activities." If students have only had directed homework assignments before, they may need help creating a weekly schedule (see example on page 153).

SOME STUDENTS MAY NEED SUGGESTIONS OF WHAT TO DO EACH DAY, NOT JUST "BY THE END OF THE WEEK, COMPLETE FOUR ACTIVITIES."

## Assessment

While these examples are designed for students in second through eighth grades, you can see how to design homework projects. Near the end of each integrated thematic unit, students receive a list of key points and a list of project choices. The key points always involve the key questions and concepts that directed the unit (see example on pages 165–66). *All* students respond to the key questions. I designed a rubric and later revised it with my students for evaluating the responses to the questions. In peer response groups, the students evaluated the responses, and I also evaluated on my own. The students usually felt the questions were easy because we had studied them throughout the unit.

The projects and questions were the choice activities; everyone waited to see which ones I included on the list. By the second year in the multiage intermediate class, students were designing their own proposals. The projects were always great fun, elaborate, and fascinating to observe. The students self-evaluated and also got class feedback. Incredible learning took place during the projects, which expanded the original lessons and made the knowledge truly transferable. Pages 167 and 168 have inquiries from two units in two different year-long themes. One year was called "Keepers of Our Earth" and the next was called "Brother Eagle, Sister Sky."

# Homework Choices: Friendship and Cooperation

## From Susie Phanton

We are beginning our study of friendship and cooperation. Please choose at least one activity from each group of choices. Put a star by the activities you do, and turn in this paper with your completed choices on Friday, October 16, or Monday, October 19.

### Writing Activities

- **Interview** a friend. Write five questions and record your friend's answers.
- **Write** a story about you and your friend.
- **Write** a letter to a friend. Address the envelope.
- **Write** a poem about a friend.

### Reading Activities

- **Read** a story about friendship, such as *Frog and Toad Are Friends.*
- **Find** and **read** some poems about friendship.

### Math Activities

- **Play** a game with a friend that involves math, such as Yahtzee, Monopoly, or Pig.
- **Make** a graph of the degree to which you and your friends like something.
- **Write** several word problems about you and your friends.

# Weekly Spelling
### From Monarch Community School

1. Students will copy their spelling words for the week on Monday.

2. Students will complete the following tasks as homework:
   - ✔ Write each word four times.
   - ✔ Study words by spelling them out loud.
   - ✔ Take a practice test at home.
   - ✔ Complete at least two of the following activities.

     - ❑ Alphabetize the words.
     - ❑ Select five words and use each in a sentence.
     - ❑ Find at least six words or the letters in magazines or newspapers; cut them out and glue them to paper.
     - ❑ Create a crossword puzzle that uses at least six of the words.
     - ❑ Use toothpicks or string and glue to construct at least five of the words on paper.
     - ❑ Use all the words in at least three sentences, and use those sentences to write a paragraph that makes sense.
     - ❑ Write five words and draw a picture that represents each word next to it.
     - ❑ Look up five words in the dictionary and write a strong definition for each.

3. Complete all tasks and turn in the work with the Friday work packet.

# Key Questions for Keepers of Our Earth: "Into the Woods"

From Monarch Community School

1. **Describe** and **illustrate** the cross-section of a tree. Label at least five growth layers and tell what their functions are.

2. **Describe** and **illustrate** at least six amazing facts about redwood trees.

3. **Compare** deciduous and evergreen trees. **Describe** or **show** at least four things that make them different.

4. **Find** and **report** the circumference and diameter of at least five things. **Describe** the steps in finding out the diameter of something.

5. **Describe** the difference between alternate and opposite leaf arrangements. **Draw** four different leaves from trees native to Santa Cruz.

6. **Describe** or **draw** at least ten products that humans use made primarily from wood.

7. **Describe** in a well-written paragraph how you collected leaves for your collection. Where did you go? What difficulties did you have? What did you discover? How did you find out the leaves' names?

# Key Questions for Brother Eagle, Sister Sky: "Sunny Days Are Here Again"

From Monarch Community School

1. **Describe** in a well-written paragraph what you know about the sun. It's okay to research or look at handouts, but respond in your own words.

2. **Tell** or **draw** what you know about a lunar eclipse. You can research this topic further if you wish.

3. **List** or **draw** things that are opaque, translucent, and transparent.

4. **Illustrate** and **label** our solar system. Include as much detail and color as you can.

5. **Describe** the key elements of a solar cooker. List at least four benefits of cooking with a solar cooker. What materials must you have? Name three kinds of solar cooker. **Draw** a solar cooker you have seen used.

6. **Complete** a graph that shows the diameters of each planet. Write at least three observations based on the information in the graph.

7. **Describe** what you liked best about this unit. On what do you wish we would have spent more time?

# Keepers of Our Earth: "Into the Woods"

From Monarch Community School

Inquiry Projects: "Mays"

In addition to *writing the essay* "What I Learned" and *answering the key questions,* choose the appropriate number of *inquiry projects* from the list below. Choose carefully and do your *personal best.*

Sea and Earth groups choose *one* project; Sky group, choose at least *two.*

1. **Create** a display of pictures and examples of various ways in which we use lumber. Cut out pictures from magazines or draw your own. Categorize and label your examples.

2. **Create** a display of early tools, techniques, and simple machines that were used for logging. Cut out pictures from magazines or draw your own. Include labels and short descriptions.

3. **Build or carve** something out of wood and bring it to school to share. Get your parents' help if you need to. Be prepared to describe the type of wood you used and the tools you needed.

4. **Make** some paper at home and bring it in. Be prepared to tell the class how you made it.

5. **Create and illustrate** a children's dictionary of at least ten forest and tree words. Use good paper and colored pencils or crayons. Spiral bind your book at school.

6. **Interview** a logger or carpenter about ways they work with timber or lumber. Write at least ten questions. Use a tape recorder or camcorder, if you can. Write up the interview to share with the class, and play your recorded version.

7. **Compose and perform** a song about trees or other things you learned during our unit. You can use a familiar tune and add your own words, if you wish.

8. **Illustrate** at least six scenes from *Little House in the Big Woods* by Laura Ingalls Wilder. Include scenes about trees or that take place in the woods. Bind your illustrations into a book, if you wish.

# Brother Eagle, Sister Sky: "Sunny Days Are Here Again"

### From Monarch Community School

In addition to *organizing your folder, writing the essay* "What I Learned," and *answering the key questions*, choose the appropriate number of *inquiry projects* from the list below. Choose carefully and do your *personal best.*

Blue group choose *one* project; red and green groups choose at least *two.*

1. **Create** a colorful poster in which you carefully illustrate the birth and death of star and at least two stages in between.

2. **Create** a mobile of the solar system.

3. **Carve, cast, or sculpt** a landscape of the Moon or Mars.

4. **Explain** why there is day and night on Earth and on other planets using words and an illustration or a demonstration.

5. **Create** an illustrated children's dictionary of at least ten space and solar system words. Use good paper and colored pencils or crayons. Spiral bind your book if you wish.

6. **Interview** an astronomer. Write ten questions, then write up the interview to present to the class.

7. **Compose and perform** a song about space or other things you learned during this unit. You can use a familiar tune and add your own words, if you wish.

8. **Investigate** a constellation of your choice. Tell who named it and why it is so named. Tell when and where we can see it. Draw the constellation.

9. **Explain** in words or pictures with labels how shadows change during the day and throughout the year.

10. **Research** the recent discoveries regarding possible life on Mars. Make a short oral report to the class.

If you have an idea of your own, submit your proposal!

# *Where to Begin*

1. Create choices in homework. Sometimes it seems overwhelming at first to orchestrate choices for a whole class to make during class time. We are often more willing and able to manage individual choices for homework activities. Determine a short list of projects or activities that might be done at home during the week. Make sure that they all can be done independently and carry, at least in your mind, equal weight or value. Make sure the instructions to the students are clear and include a cover letter to parents about your plan and expectations.

2. List extension or follow-up activities that could be the culminating projects for a unit of study. Textbooks often include such enrichment activities in the support materials. Make sure students and parents know the expectations and how they will be evaluated. It is important to keep your list short at first, and to ensure that the choices are of equal value or require equal effort.

3. If you have been doing centers at the primary level and have had complex rotation schedules, consider having some free choice time. You will need to establish appropriate procedures. Make students accountable for their choices. Perhaps they could share their experiences and choices in a brief gathering after the free choice time.

# 10
# Student Goal Setting and Self-Assessment

*Helping Them Do Their Personal Best*

## Begin with the Brain

》》 *By facilitating students' attentional focus on personal goals and immediate feedback, we can actually help their brains direct their attention by bringing these goals to a conscious level.*

Most of the attentional shifts in the brain are subconscious. However, we can purposefully shift our attention through immediate relevant feedback, discussion, focus, collaboration, visualization, and commitment. Helping ourselves and our students concentrate brain energy on specific processes and outcomes allows us to set and reach goals. A positive emotional climate and a low-stress environment allow the brain to internalize feedback and stay focused on goals. We can also customize feedback to individual students and assist them in making appropriate choices. As students begin to know their own personal strengths and challenges, they can make better choices and set realistic goals.

## Creating a Culture for Success

Do your students experience personal success every day? Do they observe others, including you, being successful? Do they routinely celebrate their successes and those of others? Does the climate in your learning environment exude an "I can do it!" feeling? Your answers to these questions will indicate whether you have fostered a positive climate and a culture that emphasizes success.

As a teacher I try to create and facilitate a culture of success in the classroom. My own positive attitude and ability to handle daily stress will be a key factor in setting the tone. Without being too much of a Pollyanna, I always point out the positive aspects of situations. My students know and understand the saying "Is your glass half full or half empty?"

I recognized this same attitude and encouragement when I was on the television game show "Hollywood Squares" years ago. I noticed that, whenever contestants made obviously ridiculous or thoughtless moves on the giant board, the charismatic host Peter Marshall wouldn't humiliate them or call attention to their blunder. He would simply say, in a matter-of-fact way, "Well, this may work out." And, incredibly, it often did! Just for the record, he never had to say it to me. I was on a nighttime version and won more than four thousand dollars in cash and prizes, including a trip to England. I missed the car by one question. Well, I guess that part didn't work out.

In a positive environment, you can foster a culture of success. In such a culture, students have positive self-concepts and self-esteem. They know, from a pattern of experiences, that even if at

DO YOUR STUDENTS EXPERIENCE PERSONAL SUCCESS EVERY DAY? DO THEY OBSERVE OTHERS, INCLUDING YOU, BEING SUCCESSFUL? DO THEY ROUTINELY CELEBRATE THEIR SUCCESSES AND THOSE OF OTHERS?

first they don't achieve a goal, they will be encouraged and given an opportunity to try again until they succeed. They also know that learning is a process through which they will construct their own understandings in multiple attempts and modifications. When people succeed immediately on every task they attempt, they are not challenged and their motivation may wane.

# Setting and Achieving Goals

You can develop the following system to assist students in setting and achieving academic and personal goals. If you implement this system routinely in your classroom, students will begin to store it as a program that they can count on to succeed in the future.

1. **Know and understand the plan or task through agendas, schedules, and assigned projects.** Students shouldn't have to be mind readers. Even to begin to set goals, students must clearly understand the expectations, time lines, and challenges involved.

   ☆ Post and review a daily agenda, and review it at the beginning of class to alert students to the tasks they are going to do on that day and in what order.

   ☆ Write up clear expectations and requirements for projects and homework assignments. If possible, send copies home to parents.

   ☆ Post procedures for tasks and review them before starting a project.

   ☆ Post or send home calendars that clearly mark events, deadlines, and benchmarks for extended projects.

   ☆ At independent centers, post the tasks and expectations in writing or identify them with symbols so all students understand the goals.

2. **Note personal relevance and connection to the curriculum content or task.** Students should have an opportunity to discover what meaning the task or curriculum selection has for them. Although the course

description and you will often determine the content of the class, students should be able to see how they can align their own needs, wants, and experiences with the instructional goals. You can often achieve this end by offering them an opportunity to choose how they can achieve the goal.

☆ Introduce the instructional goal in a way that shows students the personal relevance: link it to the here and now, relate it to their personal and social concerns, or tie it to their prior experiences.

☆ Assist students by generating an emotional bridge from their world and daily lives to the academic task. This connection can help students generate personal feelings about the topic.

☆ Ensure students understand that there will be opportunities to choose topics and projects within the instructional goals. Students may be able to choose extension activities, areas in which to become experts, or ways they will be assessed.

3. **Create opportunities and develop students' ability to analyze the task and make a plan.** Once they know the task, students need guidance in analyzing it. By analyzing the steps they need to complete successfully, the students create a game plan that includes a time line and benchmarks.

☆ As part of the initial lesson, facilitate a discussion about the sequence of steps students need to complete the task.

☆ Help students visualize what the task might look like at various benchmarks along the way.

☆ Teach students how to predict and estimate the amount of time each step will take. Plot these times on a calendar or daily schedule.

☆ Begin to develop rubrics or self-assessment surveys that help students evaluate their progress. Ask students to reflect on what a good one looks like.

4. **Determine what resources students need to complete the task. Assess the materials you have and plan to acquire necessary items you don't have.** In a truly enriched environment, many of the resources are available to students, depending, of course, on students' ages and degree of responsibility, as well as the level of support available from home.

   ☆ Based on the previous task analysis and plan, students note the supplies or resources in the classroom.

   ☆ Students will use various ways to get the materials they need outside the classroom.

   ☆ If possible, allow students to have access to the Internet, and train them in the skills necessary to gather information there.

5. **Give students accurate, timely feedback throughout the task.** Their peers, you, other adults, and the students themselves can give feedback. The evaluation should not surprise students. If you have been giving accurate feedback at several points, then students will be aware of the degree of success with which they have completed the task.

   ☆ Set up logical points within the process to give feedback. These benchmarks will probably be the same for all students. At these sessions, compliment students on what is developing well and give them constructive comments about the areas that need to improve.

   ☆ Creating a system for giving feedback is helpful. Develop a rubric for the final evaluation and use it during the project to assess progress, as well.

   ☆ Clearly define and delineate the evaluation tools to students *before* the final assessment. This measure allows students to practice self-assessment before they submit any work for feedback.

☆ It is your responsibility to create a system that provides timely, even immediate, feedback. One way to ensure timely feedback is to assess different benchmarks on different days. Rotate days on which the groups hand in their work.

☆ Make the feedback system multidynamic. In other words, ask students to do a self-assessment first, then get feedback from two peers, then submit the revised work to you.

6. **Allow process time for students to create new meaning and gain understanding.** This personal process time can allow for new understandings to sink in and for what Candace Pert (1997) refers to as "self-honesty." Students can use the time to consider possible modifications to their work.

JUST BECAUSE SOMETHING SEEMS RELEVANT TO YOU DOESN'T MEAN THAT STUDENTS WILL SEE PERSONAL CONNECTIONS IMMEDIATELY.

☆ To invoke an emotional connection to the work, give students the opportunity to discuss the process and the feedback with others in a peer review group.

☆ Just because something seems relevant to you doesn't mean that students will see personal connections immediately. Allow personal process time to allow students to link the task to prior learning and patterns.

☆ Take time to honor the work students have done and the goods things that are emerging. When you immediately suggest changes, you don't take time to recognize and allow students to savor the points they have done well.

☆ Ask students to restate feedback in their own words, writing it in a journal to help them clarify and process the comments.

# Self-Assessment

There are several ways to encourage students to self-assess their work, their behavior, their attitudes, their participation, their own understandings. They can self-reflect through journal writing, essays, group sharing, rubrics, and surveys. Younger children can use pictures to demonstrate ways in which they participated, what something looked like for them, and what they were doing during the task.

I ENCOURAGE ALL STUDENTS TO KEEP LEARNING-REFLEC- TION JOURNALS.

## Journals

I encourage all students to keep learning-reflection journals. In the journals, they do quick writings that give them a chance to process experiences and articulate goals. I prefer that they share the journal with me occasionally, so if students want to keep a private diary or journal, they do it in addition to their learning-reflection journal.

I asked my students to copy the daily agenda in their daily logs when they arrived. After they noted the tasks we would be working on, I asked them to write one or two goals for the day underneath the agenda. At the end of the day, they would go back to the agenda and check off the things they had completed and note which items they needed to finish. Then they assessed how well they had met their goals for the day and wrote a comment underneath.

## Small Process Groups

Often students can gather in groups of three to six to share their work and offer feedback to one another. The groups can be set up to give formal feedback for writing or peer response. You can also have table teams or randomly selected groups. Establish procedures for sharing, listening, and giving feedback. Group members use a rubric to guide their suggestions. Students then take the feedback and reflect in journals or by telling the group how they will use the information.

## Surveys

Sometimes I have used a checklist survey to help students self-assess. The questions help them reflect on their progress and consider what still needs to be done. A good self-survey encourages students to reflect on how well they have participated in a group's process and progress. The following example allows students to self-assess effectively.

A GOOD SELF-SURVEY ENCOURAGES STUDENTS TO REFLECT ON HOW WELL THEY HAVE PARTICIPATED IN A GROUP'S PROCESS AND PROGRESS.

### Team Member Survey

_____ 1. I felt included in the group; I felt the other members listened to me.

_____ 2. I voiced my opinions on issues and shared my ideas.

_____ 3. I accepted the various ideas and opinions that my teammates shared.

_____ 4. I accepted some of the responsibilities of the group; I did my share.

_____ 5. I shared materials with my group.

_____ 6. I completed my tasks on time; no one had to bug me to get done.

_____ 7. My teammates appreciated my efforts and thought I contributed.

_____ 8. I told others when I thought they were doing a good job; I complimented them.

_____ 9. I tried to resolve conflicts as they came up; I did not escalate problems.

_____ 10. My teammates feel that they can trust me; I show them respect.

## Rubrics

Share any rubrics or evaluation criteria with students at the onset of a task or project. This tool allows students to do the most effective self-evaluations. Rubrics have several criteria that might include content, process, mechanics, timeliness, presentation, artistic quality, and creativity (see samples on pages 179, 180, and 181). A three-point gradient will probably give younger children sufficient feedback. The middle level or number two would indicate what a basic project should look or be like. A number one would indicate that elements were missing. A number three would indicate that the project or task had all aspects completed correctly; it went beyond the original expectations.

Older students and adults seem to do better with four- or five-point rubrics. When writing the indicators for success, I always find it easiest to write the first level—that is, what an incomplete task would look like—and what the highest level would look like (see example on page 179). I complete the indicators in between later. I will often give students the indicators for the second-highest level only, then let them be creative in coming up with what an exceptional product would look like or be like.

# Multiple Intelligences

Most teachers have at least heard about Howard Gardner's (1983) multiple intelligence theory. In his search for a better way to determine human intellectual capacities, Gardner defined *intelligence* as "a set of skills of problem solving—enabling the individual to *resolve genuine problems or difficulties* that he or she encounters and, when appropriate, to create an effective product—and must also entail the potential for *finding or creating problems*—thereby laying the groundwork for the acquisition of new knowledge" (60–61).

Understanding their multiple intelligences can help students set goals and self-assess. I strongly recommend that you give all students a foundation in the theory and the language of the intelligences. Even primary students can begin to understand the concepts and competencies associated with each intelligence. Many teachers are setting up classroom centers named for the intelligences, such as the "Linguistic Station" or "Word-Smart Center."

I think Thomas Armstrong (1993, 1994, 1999) and David Lazear (1999) offer the best resources for understanding and implementing multiple intelligences. See Armstrong's revised and updated *Seven Kinds of Smart* and *Multiple Intelligences in the Classroom*, and *In Their Own Way*. Lazear's work includes *Eight Ways of Knowing* and *The Rubrics Way*. Understanding the various intelligences and their implications for teaching and learning may be the single most important step you take in your teaching career.

# Project Assessment Chart

| Assessment Area | Awesome! 1 | A Good Effort! 2 | A Work in Progress 3 | Just Beginning 4 |
|---|---|---|---|---|
| Organization | Extremely well organized<br>Easy to follow<br>Flows smoothly | Some organization<br>Most ideas flowed<br>Thoughtful arrangement<br>Occasional confusion | Somewhat unorganized<br>No flow of ideas<br>Scattered<br>Lost reader | Confusing<br>Difficult to follow<br>Lacked format<br>Ideas not coherent |
| Content Accuracy and Understanding | Comprehensive and accurate facts<br>Detailed explanations added to reader's understanding | Most facts accurate<br>A few errors in information<br>Some explanations not clearly developed | Somewhat accurate<br>Several errors in information<br>Content not researched<br>Inconsistent explanations | Most facts not accurate or researched<br>Based on assumed information; misleading |
| Comprehensive Research | Went above and beyond to research<br>Used Internet effectively<br>Used six or more resources | Utilized a variety of resources<br>Did research out of class<br>Used four or more resources | Used most of the resources provided in an acceptable manner<br>No evidence of consulting outside resources | Ineffective use of resources<br>Did little or nor research<br>No evidence of research |
| Presentation and Mechanics | Ideas presented in a unique manner<br>Impeccable mechanics<br>Engaging! | Ideas presented in an effective manner<br>A few mechanical errors | At times some ideas presented clearly<br>Many mechanical errors<br>Seemed in draft form rather than final | Lacked effective presentation qualities<br>Ideas unclear<br>Serious mechanical errors<br>First draft quality |
| Creativity | Clever and unique<br>Original ideas enhanced total project<br>Artwork and other elements add a great deal of interest | Thoughtfully presented<br>Artwork and other elements add interest | Few original touches to enhance project<br>Basic artwork and other elements<br>Obviously didn't spend time developing | Predictable<br>Just covered the basics<br>No artwork or other elements to add interest |

# Integrated Curriculum—Sample Student Rubric

| Assessment Area | Evidence Not Yet Observed 1 | Need More Time and Support 2 | Appropriate Development 3 | Secure, Strong Performance 4 |
|---|---|---|---|---|
| Unit Concepts _____ _____ _____ | | | | |
| Content Knowledge and Understanding _____ _____ _____ | | | | |
| Competencies and Skills _____ _____ _____ | | | | |
| Use of Technology _____ _____ _____ | | | | |
| Authentic Assessment _____ _____ _____ | | | | |

# Integrated Curriculum—Assessment of Teacher-Developed Units

| Assessment Area | Emergent Implementation 1 | 2 | 3 | Fluent Implementation 4 |
|---|---|---|---|---|
| Dynamic Content and Concepts | Content not original. Some concepts not developmentally appropriate. Lacks research data. Little or no local firsthand connection. | | | Rich, researched content. Interesting to students of this age. Concepts developmentally appropriate. Strong local, relevant connections. |
| Planning and Organization | Format not clear. A collection of unlinked activities. Many parts not yet developed. Inconsistent pattern of organization. | | | Extremely well organized; logical format. Includes all aspects of quality curriculum writing. Organization enhances implementation. |
| Instructional Strategies | Poor variety of strategies. Relies on traditional whole group teaching. Limited student participation. Few firsthand experiences. | | | Includes a range of appropriate instructional strategies: flex, groups, firsthand, research. Maintains high student involvement. |
| Integration of Content Area | Curriculum taught as separate subjects. Infrequent integration opportunities. Some interdisciplinary connections. | | | Fully integrates content, concepts, and competencies within most experiences. Connections are made to real world. |
| Integration of Technology | Use of technology not a regular part of the unit. Basic word processing, graphs, commercial software occasionally implemented. | | | Multiple uses of technology throughout unit. Innovative strategies and creative ideas for student use. |
| Competencies and Skills | Skills taught in isolation or not at all. Students not given opportunities to develop specific competencies. | | | Skills and competencies are taught within the context of the project or activity. Multiple opportunities to develop abilities and processes. |
| Assessment Strategies | No student assessment strategies for unit or basic traditional methods only. Little alignment with district and state 3 Cs. | | | Various assessment strategies included. Authentic projects and performances used to evaluate and document student learning. |

As students begin to understand their own natural strengths, they will know why they are drawn to certain types of activities and projects. They will also begin to understand why some tasks seem so challenging. In most cases, students find tasks demanding that require them to use an intelligence they have not yet developed. By understanding their areas of expertise, students will be able to select activities and set learning goals that they are more likely to meet. When assigned a challenging task, students may discover ways they can utilize personal strengths to succeed. Mastering multiplication facts, for example, may be easier for bodily-kinesthetic learners if they can jump rope or dance while memorizing.

I use a self-assessment survey to help students see which intelligences they seem to be developing and which ones they have not yet developed. I do *not* test them to label them, or to determine what they can and can't do. The test is only a survey that may identify current strengths. By knowing these strengths, they can more confidently set goals.

I know, for example, that I have very strong interpersonal and bodily-kinesthetic intelligences. If given choices of ways to complete a task, I always choose working with others and creating a presentation or performance. By making that choice, I increase the likelihood of my success, based on my past experiences and my understanding of my own intelligences.

Give the generic checklists on pages 184–86 to your students to use as a self-assessment. The ten statements for each of the intelligences are written from a child's perspective. Many more indicators exist. Send the survey home with younger students, and ask their parents to assist them in reading and responding. Remember that there isn't a final score in each area. In fact, it is important to remember that marking as many as four or five out of ten items under each intelligence could indicate your flexibility and aptitude for using all intelligences. You are not limited in any way!

When I first gave students at the Monarch Community School the MI checklist I developed, I was surprised by the results. I had already been teaching them about multiple intelligences for some time. They recognized their strengths and understood my effort to teach using as many intelligences as possible. When the first surveys were returned, I noticed that students had checked off almost every item in every category. I thought they were playing a joke on me. When I asked them to explain, these fourth-, fifth-, and sixth-grade students said that because they were consciously being encouraged to develop *all* their intelligences, they felt as though they could do almost everything mentioned on the checklist. They felt empowered as opposed to limited!

## *Where to Begin*

1. Model daily goal setting with your students by sharing an agenda with them, then assessing at the end of the day or lesson whether or not you accomplished your goals.

2. Begin to offer choices that address all eight intelligences in your teaching. Help your students become aware of their own strengths and areas that are developing.

3. Ask students to begin keeping daily journals in which they record the agenda and note their own goals for the day. Allow time at the end of the day or at the end of each lesson for self-reflection, processing, and assessment.

# Eight Kinds of Smart
## Student Checklist

Multiple intelligences include common skills that people have and that they use to process information and solve problems. Which are your strongest intelligences and your least developed? Check those statements that apply to you most often to find out.

### Verbal-Linguistic: Word Smart

____ Books are important to me.
____ I have a pretty easy time memorizing poems, stories, facts, and so on.
____ I enjoy talking and telling stories.
____ I enjoy games such as Scrabble, Boggle, and hangman.
____ I like to write in a journal or to write stories.
____ I like to look things up in books and encyclopedias.
____ I like to listen to people read aloud to me.
____ When I ride in a car, I like to read signs or play the ABC game.
____ I enjoy tongue twisters, rhymes, and puns.
____ I like to use big words when I write or speak.

### Logical-Mathematical: Logic Smart

____ I enjoy counting things.
____ I like to make patterns and I notice patterns in the world.
____ I often ask adults questions about the way things work.
____ I can add and subtract in my head.
____ I like to measure, sort, and organize things.
____ I like to play games or solve problems that require logical thinking.
____ I am interested in new inventions and theories in science.
____ I like to set up little experiments.
____ I enjoy doing math at school.
____ I like watching science shows on TV.

### Visual-Spatial: Picture Smart

____ I enjoy drawing and painting pictures and designs.
____ I love colors and I have some special favorites.
____ I enjoy putting together puzzles.
____ I like playing with blocks, Legos, Tinker Toys, and so on.
____ I have vivid and colorful dreams.

_____ I can close my eyes and visualize things in my head.

_____ I can usually find my way around my neighborhood or town.

_____ I like to take pictures or videos.

_____ I love to look at picture books or magazines that have a lot of photographs.

_____ I can pick and match clothes to create great outfits.

## Bodily-Kinesthetic: Body Smart

_____ I play at least one sport on a regular basis.

_____ I find it difficult to sit still for long periods of time.

_____ I like working with my hands, doing activities such as building, weaving, carving, and so on.

_____ I am well coordinated.

_____ I need to touch things to learn more about them.

_____ I love wild rides at the amusement park and other thrilling experiences.

_____ I often spend my free time outside.

_____ I like to ride a bike, skateboard, or skate.

_____ I enjoy dancing. I can act out things and imitate other people's movements.

## Musical-Rhythmic: Music Smart

_____ I have a pretty good singing voice.

_____ I can tell when someone sings or plays a wrong or off-key note.

_____ I like to play or would like to learn to play a musical instrument.

_____ I like to listen to music on the radio, or on CDs or audiocassettes.

_____ I sometimes catch myself humming a tune when I am working or learning.

_____ I love to have music in my life.

_____ I like to tap or bang on things to keep up a rhythm.

_____ I've actually made up some of my own songs or music.

_____ I notice nonverbal sounds (dogs barking, waves breaking, and so on) and hear things pretty well.

_____ I sometimes get a melody or advertisement jingle stuck in my head.

## Naturalist: Nature Smart

_____ I love nature, animals, and the outdoors.

_____ I can sense and notice patterns in nature; I enjoy pointing them out to others.

_____ I am able to use patterns to navigate (get around); I am not afraid of getting lost in nature or a new environment.

_____ I am sensitive to the changes in seasons, moon phases, tides, star patterns, and so on.

_____ I am interested in learning the names and characteristics of various plants and animals.

_____ I enjoy watching nature shows and shows about exploration and cultures different from my own.

_____ I find it fascinating, not frightening, to be in environments different from my own.

_____ I enjoy watching natural phenomena such as comets, sunsets, thunderstorms, and waves.

_____ I blend in easily with nature or a new culture; sometimes I feel more comfortable in those environments than in my own.

_____ I often want to be out in nature when I am thinking about something or solving a problem.

## Interpersonal: People Smart

_____ I usually have an easy time making friends.

_____ I am a good at helping others solve problems.

_____ I often want to help others.

_____ I usually know what is going on with my friends and family.

_____ I am often a leader in clubs or cooperative learning groups.

_____ I am the kind of person who others seem to come to for advice.

_____ I prefer group sports to individual ones.

_____ I like playing games with others more than playing individual games.

_____ I feel comfortable in crowds and at social gatherings.

_____ I notice when people are upset or having a hard time.

## Intrapersonal: Self Smart

_____ I am pretty independent; I don't rely that much on others.

_____ I have hobbies that I like to do on my own.

_____ Sometimes I have opinions or ideas that set me apart from others.

_____ I like to keep a diary or journal.

_____ I prefer spending time alone in the woods to spending time at a busy, fancy resort.

_____ I prefer playing games by myself (video games, solitaire) to playing with others.

_____ I have some important ideas or goals that I like to think about.

_____ I need time to work on things by myself rather than in a cooperative group.

_____ I have a secret place or fort to which I retreat to get away from others.

_____ I sometimes have a difficult time talking with others in a small group.

# 11
# Student Acknowledgment and Recognition

*Providing Accurate Feedback and Organizing Learning Celebrations*

## Begin with the Brain

*Behaviorists taught us that we could increase positive behaviors by reinforcing through rewards, and reduce negative behaviors by ignoring or giving consequences. Current research suggests that the brain is capable of making its own rewards. By producing and releasing natural opiates and endorphins, the brain can create a natural high.*

Humans consistently seek new experiences and are curious without needing external rewards. The brain begins to produce pleasurable feelings when accomplishing a task, enjoying an activity, succeeding, sharing affection, laughing, or being entertained. The brain self-satisfies by seeking out novelty and challenge. If students are in a threatening environment, then the brain releases chemicals such as cortisol, adrenaline, and vasopressin, which generate a survival response and possible anger and aggression. In brain-based, learner-centered classrooms, orchestrate opportunities for the brain to generate intrinsic motivation. Provide ample feedback and acknowledgment, and celebrate learning; rely less on external rewards and motivators.

# Weaning Off Rewards

REWARDS, LIKE PUN-
ISHMENTS, CAN ONLY
MANIPULATE SOME-
ONE'S ACTIONS. THEY
DO NOTHING TO HELP A
CHILD BECOME A KIND
OR CARING PERSON.
— ALFIE KOHN

To establish brain-compatible learning environments, we must wean our students off rewards and outright bribery! While I used to think upper-grade students were the only ones trained to expect rewards, I now realize that our kindergarten students arrive already programmed into working and performing for extrinsic rewards. Obviously, many parents give rewards. But the pattern worsens in school, perhaps simply with stars and stickers in primary classrooms. As kids get a little older, it seems to grow into pizza parties and privileges. By middle school the stakes get higher, and parents continue to fall into the trap by giving monetary rewards for grades. Children and many adults are terribly dependent on what compensation they will receive for their compliance or performance. But internal motivation decreases as the drive for external rewards increases.

Eric Jensen (1996) defines a reward as "a compensation or consequence which is both: 1. predictable and 2. has market value" (234). But what Jensen doesn't mention is that a reward may cause the learners to change their behavior or do something to get the reward; when the reward is gone, they revert back to the old behavior. As Alfie Kohn (1996) describes reward systems, they do not promote meaningful learning or intrinsic motivation: "Rewards, like punishments, can only manipulate someone's actions. They do nothing to help a child become a kind or caring person" (34).

Occasionally, it's okay to offer incentives for short-term compliance, for instance if we need to get something done quickly. On a day-to-day basis, though, we must provide only acknowledgment and recognition for students' efforts and successes. We also need to orchestrate learning celebrations that include parents. These family gatherings will provide the emotional and social recognition that students can use to affirm their efforts and success.

Take some time to discuss with students why you are gradually phasing out the reward systems and what your new expectations are. Then allow reward systems you have used to gradually disappear. For instance, many students are "addicted" to stamps or stickers on their written work and papers. When I finally decided not to put stars on their pages, I created a *self-serve station*. The station was a small metal box that had all the miscellaneous stickers and stamps I had collected. If students felt that they deserved a visual reward when they got a paper back, they could go choose one and put it on for themselves. This replacement method served many purposes:

☆ Students looked a little harder at the comments from me on work to see if they should have a sticker.

☆ Within weeks, the box was almost forgotten, with only a few students still going to it regularly. The stickers from the box seemed to have become unnecessary and time consuming.

☆ Eventually only those students who recognized that their piece of work was an exceptional effort or performance went and put on their own form of acknowledgment and affirmation. They were in transition!

# Meaningful Feedback as Acknowledgment

To acknowledge our achievements and effort, we seek feedback from several sources and in several ways. The hardest part of all the techniques is allowing for the time! It is so easy to push the time limit to the very end of class and simply *not* have the time to process, reflect, and give feedback. We really should begin to consider feedback time as the key point of the whole lesson.

## Interaction, Process, or Experience

If you design learning activities to include real experiences, there will be lots of opportunities for immediate feedback. As students do experiments, discovery play, or attempt to solve problems, the reactions and effects they observe while doing the activity will provide ample feedback. Trial and error is extremely motivating to someone who is working on a task.

Give students many opportunities to have experiences that teach and reward through the experience itself. In primary classrooms, set up choice centers to encourage building, creating, sewing, computing. These activities provide daily opportunities for children to find out how things work. Getting to build with blocks or Legos gives students immediate feedback: if something doesn't look the way they want it or falls over, then students have to keep trying to get it right, which motivates them. When they complete a project, they have a real sense of accomplishment. In intermediate classrooms, allow students to work with similar items that are more age appropriate. They might create electric circuits to light bulbs and make bells go off, or build an irrigation system for the class garden. If students get stuck, they may ask for some adult feedback, but more often than not, you will find students deeply focused on something they are trying to figure out, making modifications and forging onward.

I remember a time when my students were working on creating solar cookers out of pizza boxes. They had to create an insulated oven, cover the surface with smooth aluminum foil, then design a

TRIAL AND ERROR IS EXTREMELY MOTIVATING TO SOMEONE WHO IS WORKING ON A TASK.

way to adjust the reflective surface so it heated the cooking area. We went through a lot of foil, masking tape, string, and cardboard that day, but the various completed designs were incredible. The adult leaders gave the students very little feedback. The students understood the concepts and had the resources and time they needed. Their level of concentration and motivation was extremely high. And quite honestly, the lukewarm hot dogs and quesadillas with only slightly melted cheese never tasted any better than they did that day!

Although I tend to resist allowing students to work on computers for routine tasks that they can do with other materials at school, many software programs give wonderful immediate feedback. As an example, the Mavis Beacon Teaches Typing and the Mario Typing programs are interactive enough that students really work to improve their keyboarding skills; as they improve their scores, they move on to the next level. Such scores and achievements are incentives and motivators, but really not rewards since they have no market value.

## Self-Reflection

As we help students learn how to gather feedback, we can model for them how to self-reflect. Something as simple as reviewing the daily agenda at the end of the day and noting which items you completed and which ones need more time can show them how to self-reflect. Occasionally, I have reviewed some of their work and decided to modify a strategy or lesson I was using. I always share such decisions with them so they know I constantly look at my own work as a teacher, just as I want them to look at theirs as students. Tell them when you are noting what goes on around you and reflecting on decisions or modifications.

I think the greatest reason students don't know how to self-reflect is that we haven't given them time to do so and to process their experiences. It is during this mental rehearsal and reflection that greater understanding can occur. An excellent way for students to begin self-reflection is by keeping journals. After they complete an activity or at points during the process, ask them to write a

I THINK THE GREATEST REASON STUDENTS DON'T KNOW HOW TO SELF-REFLECT IS THAT WE HAVEN'T GIVEN THEM TIME TO DO SO AND TO PROCESS THEIR EXPERIENCES.

191

little in their journals. Provide some frame sentences such as those that follow as writing prompts.

- ☆ I think this project is going well because
- ☆ The hardest part of this work was
- ☆ If I do this kind of activity again, I think I will
- ☆ The thing I wish I knew before I started was
- ☆ If I were going to show this to someone, I would share it with _____ because

As I said in the previous chapter, give students access to any assessment criteria you are using, such as a copy of a rubric. If they have the information in advance, they can determine whether they are meeting the criteria at the desired level.

## Feedback from Peers

In a learner-centered classroom, the trusting relationships that are formed will be the foundation for peer feedback. Remember that we usually aren't willing to hear ideas or be influenced by someone with whom we have no relationship or sense of trust. Set up procedures so that peers can safely give each other accurate, meaningful feedback.

The easiest way to start peer feedback is by assigning partners. Students pair with other students whom they already know and trust. They share writings or drawings that they have completed and ask partners to give them two compliments and one suggestion. I usually call this process "one to grow on." When students give feedback about stories and creative writing, give them a specific framework for the type of critique they are doing. For instance, when they read the story, are they supposed to be checking spelling or just noting if it makes sense? Maybe they are just supposed to give feedback about whether or not the author's name is on the paper, the pages are in order, and stapled together. Be sure they know so they don't waste time or fail to do what you want them to do.

Another good method for introducing students to peer feedback is to have some students serve as peer tutors or classroom experts. Many teachers of multiage classes use this technique. If you have students who have already mastered certain tasks or concepts, tell other students who they are; those who need help can ask them for feedback. This process saves you a lot of time, as well, because students don't see you as the only expert in the classroom. I post a sign in my room that says "Ask three, then me!" to remind students to ask three of their peers, then me if they still don't have helpful feedback.

In *Teaching with the Brain in Mind,* Eric Jensen (1998) notes, "While there may be little 'hard biological research' on the value of cooperative groups, clearly they do two important things. When we feel valued and cared for, our brain releases the neurotransmitters of pleasure: endorphins and dopamine. This helps us enjoy our work more. Another positive is that groups provide a superb vehicle for social and academic feedback" (33). You'll already have various groups set up in the classroom; there will be many other opportunities for students to get peer responses. Encourage table teams to give feedback. In their writing workshops they can get feedback, editing assistance, and encouragement about stories they are writing.

It is your job to model what respectful, accurate, meaningful feedback looks like and sounds like. It is also your job to help students as they learn how to deliver constructive criticism. I provide students with a list of what I call "Socratic questions" and statements that they can also use to generate a greater understanding of someone's work, presentation, or ideas.

IT IS YOUR JOB TO MODEL WHAT RESPECTFUL, ACCURATE, MEANINGFUL FEEDBACK LOOKS LIKE AND SOUNDS LIKE. IT IS ALSO YOUR JOB TO HELP STUDENTS AS THEY LEARN HOW TO DELIVER CONSTRUCTIVE CRITICISM.

### Socratic Questions

*What examples can you give to show what you mean here?*

*I wonder if what you are saying is*

*What is your reason for saying that?*

*Help me understand what you mean here.*

*Could you clarify that comment?*

*Why do you believe that?*

*How do you know that?*

We can also model and note for students when we as teachers seek feedback for ourselves. At the end of lessons or activities, I will gather the class together and ask them, "What did you like?" "What parts of the lesson worked well?" "What aspects of the lesson do you think I need to change for next time?"

## Feedback from Teachers or Other Experts

It is often difficult to create ways for us to give meaningful, immediate feedback to all students on a regular basis. We know that often the simplest response from us can go a long way. Many students just need brief acknowledgment and encouragement to keep them going. In reality only a few might be able to tolerate a long feedback session. In fact, a stressed learner, especially if in a survival response mode, will prefer feedback after she has calmed down.

But one key aspect of teacher feedback is that it should happen while the student is working on a project or a task so the student still has time to modify the product based on the new information. Nothing is more frustrating than finishing a project and finding out that you were off base right from the beginning. If students get feedback only in the form of an evaluation at the end of a project, they may not find it meaningful; they might just look at the grade and are likely to forget whatever you said for the next time.

As you rotate during a work period, give feedback to several students. Use words and written comments. Or you can often ask a table group to leave work out on their desks one afternoon each week so you have only five or six students' work to respond to. I try to have small groups rotate to work with me every day so that I have the opportunity to check in and redirect them, if necessary.

## Written Feedback

When conducting mini-conferences with students about something they are doing on paper, ask permission to write on their work before you make marks or comments. Ask them to attach that copy to whatever final work they turn in so that you can note the improvements and changes. Older children can write the feedback and corrections themselves. Hand them your "fancy pen" with which to do it and they will feel an extra sense of acknowledgment and affirmation.

## Score as You Go

When reviewing students' work such as responses to questions or math problems and computations, if an answer is correct, mark it immediately. My colleague Robert Ellingsen is a master at this. As students ask for help or feedback, he draws a star or smile on everything correct he sees or all the parts that are going well. The students know immediately that they have been successful, they feel an immediate sense of accomplishment, and they are motivated to continue with the rest of the assignment. Also, he doesn't have a stack of work because, when students turn in their papers, a large part of their work has already been evaluated.

## Work Folders

For many activities, ask students to bring or create folders to hold their works in progress. We often create a response chart that we attach to the front of the folders. On the chart are lines where I put the date and a comment along with my initials. The chart serves as a record sheet for any work that I am reviewing. I also encourage students to take the folders home and ask their parents to indicate that they reviewed the work with their children.

An easy way to make a folder is to use a 9-by-12-inch manila envelope. Lift up the flap on the back side. Cut down each of the side edges about two inches and fold the clasp edge into the folder. Moisten the flap, fold it down, and seal it to the exposed top. The students write their names in large letters on the flap. The envelope is now a nifty pocket folder to keep papers in and pass in for a check.

### Talk It Out

Although you may often be rushed and give quick feedback, be sure to allow students time to explain what they are doing. Be sure to ask them to talk themselves through their thinking. This strategy is a perfect way to help them learn self-reflection skills. Although they might think that the ideas are coming from you, be sure to point out the ways in which they are thinking for themselves!

### Rotate Feedback

To keep from being overwhelmed with student work that needs feedback, rotate which group you work with each day. I found this method especially helpful when I wanted to respond to them in their journals. I would do one table team each day. The groups knew which day of the week to leave their folders or journals on their desks. I was able to respond to everyone at least once a week.

### Verbal and Nonverbal

Don't forget how powerful and important nonverbal gestures and quick verbal affirmations can be! I use high fives often, and the students helped me create a plethora of variations on the basic hand slap! I would occasionally put my hands on a student's head to perform a "Vulcan Mind-Transfer" that I had invented. It meant that this student was being so smart that I wanted to get some of the intelligence transferred to my own brain. Use a "thumbs-up" sign from across a room.

When giving quick verbal feedback, don't overuse praise statements such as "good," "super," "okay!" "better!" and "well done!" I create my own statements, smile, and make eye contact when I say them; what a great affirmation for students. "Now you're cooking!" "I can see you are really getting into this!" "This is blowing me away!" "I don't think I've ever seen anything like this!" "Did you do this? Wow!" "*I'm impressed!*"

You can offer even constructive criticism or a little nudge in short humorous statements that convey your suggestion: "Is this your personal best today?" "I was wondering what you've been up to."

"Hmm, so you must be really thinking about what you're doing over the weekend, huh?" "I wonder what else is on your mind today?" "Do you think you can spare a little more energy to finish this correctly?"

I'll leave this section by giving you a few of Eric Jensen's (1996) thoughts on feedback: "The brain thrives on feedback: the more often, the better; the more immediate, the better; the greater the specificity, the better; the more appropriately dramatic, the better; the longer the feedback is delayed, the less useful" (285).

# Recognizing Student Effort and Achievement

## Authentic Achievement

Learner-centered classrooms will be noticeably different in many ways. The methods used to assess and evaluate will include many types of products and performances along with the more traditional methods. Designing genuine activities for the students to complete will increase their motivation and the meaning they find in their learning. Instead of giving tasks that go nowhere, that nobody sees, and that the student doesn't value, give evaluations that are authentic, that require the students to do something logical and that arise from the knowledge itself. For example ask students to build something, design brochures and newsletters, write press releases, paint murals, provide community service, design posters, orchestrate a celebration, create a museum of artwork or projects, send letters to corporations, invent something, plant and maintain a garden, clean up a river—the list is endless.

When students complete these types of projects, you may or may not evaluate their final efforts. You should, however, take regular opportunities to recognize their efforts through assemblies, achievement certificates, news releases, school newsletters, photograph displays, or even simple words of appreciation at a classroom gathering. Students will appreciate the recognition, but they will have already had the feedback to know in their minds and hearts how meaningful and successful they have been. This additional acknowledgment is meant to honor them, thank them, and provide an opportunity to inspire others to produce the types of projects their peers are doing. It can build an awareness of the depth of someone's involvement and commitment that the class may not otherwise have known about.

## Impromptu Recognition

You can plan an event to recognize someone's efforts, success, or achievements. But the more common and easiest recognition to orchestrate is impromptu. During a work period, perhaps you notice three students working very hard, above and beyond the call of duty. Before dismissing for recess, take a moment to ask them to stand or simply put your hand on their shoulders and publicly make a short statement about their degree of work and success. Some classes applaud, others snap their fingers. Lately I've seen students imitate the way you honor musicians and celebrities, by pushing palms upward in the air several times, as if they were raising the roof. A great high five in front of the class can go a long way, too.

YOU SHOULD NOTE THE EFFORTS EVEN OF THOSE STUDENTS WHO ARE NOT AT THE TOP OF THE CLASS.

You might try something other than public commendation for a consistently good effort or a spontaneous change of behavior and cooperation. I often invite students to eat lunch with me. Even older students find it a real treat. Of course, we don't just eat lunch! We put on some of their favorite rock 'n' roll music, and I always have something for a special dessert, usually juice ice pops kept in the staff refrigerator. Look for special efforts or adjustments in behavior, and once a week or so, invite a few students to lunch. You can ensure that all students will get the opportunity.

I have had a few students who didn't understand why other students were getting to have lunch with me. I took the opportunity to point out exactly what I thought the students' efforts were and the qualities I thought they had demonstrated. Eventually some of the students who didn't understand at first would point out to me when they were "being good"! Their awareness of what behavior would gain my appreciation and recognition was just beginning for these students.

## Achievement Awards

A certificate, ribbon, or award of some kind can be a treasured lifetime keepsake. I know I still have a box full of tokens I received while in school. You'll phase out many competitive events, such as math races, spelling bees, poetry contests, athletic competitions, and science fairs. While many students enjoy the external motivators these types of events create, such activities usually have the same students winning all the time, with *a lot* of "losers." If students aren't gifted in a particular area, there isn't a chance for them ever to be acknowledged, even if they are making great progress. You should note the efforts even of those students who are not at the top of the class.

REGULAR, FREQUENT ACHIEVEMENT AWARD CEREMONIES CAN BE A WAY TO PAY PUBLIC RECOGNITION TO STUDENTS WHO HAVE BEEN SUCCESSFUL AND ARE GAINING GROUND IN CERTAIN AREAS.

Regular, frequent achievement award ceremonies can be a way to pay public recognition to students who have been successful and are gaining ground in certain areas. A simple certificate, signed and dated by a respected adult, given with a handshake in a public forum, is a special event for many students (and parents)! Determining descriptors for the awards will be the key. Rather than a generic math award, perhaps recognize someone's achievement in problem solving, effort, or analysis. Instead of certificates for spelling, consider certificates for achievement in accuracy, communication skills, or perseverance. The life skills for success described in the next section are a terrific resource for the types of skills, behaviors, and competencies for which we would like to give achievement awards to our students.

# Life Skills for Success

In the midst of the controversy about whether or not schools should teach values of any kind, Dorothy Rich (1988) published *MegaSkills.* The book sent a powerful message to parents and educators about the skills beyond the three Rs that all children need to be successful beyond school: "MegaSkills are the very basic values, attitudes, and behaviors that determine a child's achievements" (back cover) The set of top ten skills that Rich recommends includes confidence, motivation, effort, responsibility, initiative, perseverance, caring, teamwork, common sense, and problem solving.

In 1991, Thomas Lickona, a well-known psychologist and religious educator, published *Educating for Character: How Our Schools Can Teach Respect and Responsibility,* in which he echoes what Rich and others continue to say: teaching very basic life skills to our children is *everyone's* responsibility, and doing so is necessary to ensure that we build a decent, humane society. In 1997, members of the research and guidelines committee of the Collaborative for the Advancement of Social and Emotional Learning (CASEL) at the University of Illinois wrote *Promoting Social and Emotional Learning: Guidelines for Educators.* CASEL's whole purpose is "to support schools and families in their efforts to educate knowledgeable, responsible, and caring young people who will become productive workers and contributing citizens in the twenty-first century" (viii). Obviously, many believe that teaching students life skills is vital.

We can and should teach the life skills in learner-centered classrooms through orchestrated lessons and activities; teaching them also means noting and recognizing through awards and celebrations our students who exhibit them. While such a list is never finite, I have assimilated various lists into the following generic list of skills, values, attitudes, and behaviors to serve us in the classroom as a set of guidelines. *Respect* and *responsibility* need to be at the top of the list. The remaining skills can arguably be placed in any order, as long as they are not presented as a hierarchy.

WE CAN AND SHOULD TEACH THE LIFE SKILLS IN LEARNER-CENTERED CLASSROOMS THROUGH ORCHESTRATED LESSONS AND ACTIVITIES.

# Life Skills for Success

| | |
|---|---|
| **Respect** | To honor self, others, and the environment |
| **Responsibility** | To be accountable for own actions |
| **Loyalty** | To be devoted and faithful to family, friends, and country |
| **Peace** | To be calm and serene, not quarrelsome or violent |
| **Cooperation** | To work together toward a common goal or purpose |
| **Integrity** | To be honest, upright, and of sound moral principle and character |
| **Kindness** | To be gentle and thoughtful toward others |
| **Initiative** | To do something because it needs to be done |
| **Flexibility** | To have the ability to alter plans when necessary |
| **Perseverance** | To continue in spite of difficulties |
| **Organization** | To plan, arrange, and implement in an orderly way |
| **Sense of humor** | To laugh and be playful without hurting others |
| **Effort** | To try your hardest and work tirelessly |
| **Reliability** | To be trustworthy and dependable |
| **Self-control** | To have command over own actions and feelings |
| **Common sense** | To use good judgment |
| **Problem solving** | To create or seek solutions in difficult situations |
| **Decision making** | To have strategies for making up one's mind and forming opinions |
| **Motivation** | To want to do something and to be willing to move into action |
| **Patience** | To wait calmly for someone or something |
| **Friendship** | To make and keep a friend through mutual trust and caring |
| **Curiosity** | To desire to learn or know about a full range of things |
| **Citizenship** | To behave as a supportive, contributing member of a country or community |

# Schoolwide Programs

Many schools have created programs that recognize students who demonstrate the life skills for success. Some have an assembly once a month to honor students whom teachers have nominated because they have consistently or recently demonstrated the skill that was being emphasized that month. Often a school counselor, vice principal, or an activities director organizes the selected skills for the whole year. In the first month of school, they might emphasize friendship, initiative, or motivation. During December, before the winter vacation, schools often emphasize kindness, citizenship, cooperation, and peace, and encourage community service and family connections. At the end of the school year, they might find that perseverance, sense of humor, and self-control are the most relevant! By dividing the skills over the school year, teachers can select two to four students each month who deserve recognition and acknowledgment in that area. By the end of the year, *all* students will have received a certificate in at least one awards assembly.

Some teachers worry that there may not be a category for the students who present a challenge. I always find that there is at least *one* month (or one life skill) in which students show their talents or expertise. It often becomes the skills in which they are most naturally talented, perhaps those that have landed them in trouble a few times, such as sense of humor, creativity, or curiosity. (I know this because my two sons seem to often fall into these categories!)

# Learning Celebrations

When students work hard to create authentic achievements, they are anxious to have friends and family view their efforts and help celebrate their work. At the end of in-depth thematic units, I orchestrate a culminating event, performance, or family gathering that marks the unit and gives students public acknowledgment for their efforts.

## Culminating Events

Usually I envision a possible culminating event first; it helps me orchestrate the whole unit, including project choices and the assessment activity. Any activity that publicly showcases student work and effort can serve as a culminating event to celebrate learning.

### *Possible Culminating Events*

*information fairs*
*museums*
*art shows*
*plays*
*how-to stations*
*armchair travel trips*
*miniature workshops*
*invention conventions*
*learning expos*
*discovery exploratorium*

As I noted earlier, one of the more popular types of learning celebrations in my intermediate multiage class was a fair. The marine mammal fair was a terrific example of multiage teams of students working together to create a booth, brochures, items to sell, information packets, logos, and drawings of a marine mammal that they had selected for their in-depth study. The intense activity and commitment from students builds almost into a frenzy of learning and production in the days before the event. You know students are hooked when they ask to stay after school to work on stuff, or arrange to go over to others' homes on weekends to work on the booth. I am always reminded of old Andy Hardy movies with Mickey Rooney and Judy Garland. My students seem just as inspired, like they are putting on a "show in the barn"!

Other popular events are museums and exploratoriums. At these events, the students have usually created products or works of art to display. They rehearse and serve as docents at the museum, giving short, informative tours. We have had interactive stations, and students have occasionally charged visiting parents a quarter to learn how to do the skill or the activity. Who wouldn't want to pay a quarter to learn how to shake cream in a glass jar to make butter?

## Performances

I highly recommend putting on a play a year. Perhaps it's my own love of the theater and performance, but I know that most children love an opportunity to at least be a part of a play or musical performance. I try to select short plays that have something to do with the topics we are studying. You can shorten longer plays, but narrate parts to link the action together. Your students can adapt many stories and novels to the theater. Make sure everyone is involved in some way: costumes, props, sets, programs, and tickets (even if you don't charge for it!). As the performance date nears, rehearsal will take up more and more class time. Be prepared and remember that the skills the students learn and experience may be more than you can teach them for the whole year.

The experience of performing in front of parents and the community is a memorable one that will last students a lifetime. The applause, recognition, laughter, mistakes, exhaustion—all of it—constitute feedback that their brains will thrive on. As in many other experiences, the process is the point. The process involved in organizing student performances is incredible, and the final product can be incredibly rewarding.

## Family Gatherings

At least three times a year, I organize a family gathering that may or may not also be a learning celebration. At the beginning of school, even before an official back-to-school night, I encourage teachers and some helpful parents to organize a potluck, a burrito bash, a barbecue, or a dessert-a-thon. At these events, my only real expectation is that families have a chance to get to know one another. It is often the first time that children can introduce their friends to their parents. I encourage *both* parents in divorced situations to come and get to know other families who are perhaps in similar circumstances.

There's no question that these events will always be above and beyond the call of our duties as the students' teacher. I have always felt that the extra effort needed to organize them only contributed to my abilities to communicate with parents and my overall understanding of the students I was serving. Well worth my time, I've always thought. It is also a chance for me to bring my own family!

By the end of the year, families know each other and have a sense of community. They look forward to coming to the end-of-year gathering. You experience the acknowledgment of your own continued efforts through the many hugs, handshakes, positive comments, and thank-yous these very grateful parents bestow upon you. They will have recognized the powerful program on which you worked so hard. They will see differences in their children. They will want to know, "Why couldn't school have been like this when I was a kid?"

The answer is simple. We are learning more and more about learning theory and the brain's capabilities. Good teachers have used many of these strategies for years. We now have the research to support, guide, and encourage us to orchestrate learner-centered classrooms with the brain in mind!

THE EXPERIENCE OF PERFORMING IN FRONT OF PARENTS AND THE COMMUNITY IS A MEMORABLE ONE THAT WILL LAST STUDENTS A LIFETIME. THE APPLAUSE, RECOGNITION, LAUGHTER, MISTAKES, EXHAUSTION—ALL OF IT— CONSTITUTE FEEDBACK THAT THEIR BRAINS WILL THRIVE ON.

## *Where to Begin*

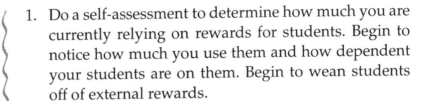

1. Do a self-assessment to determine how much you are currently relying on rewards for students. Begin to notice how much you use them and how dependent your students are on them. Begin to wean students off of external rewards.

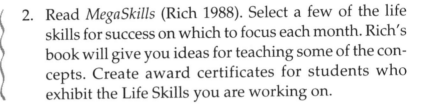

2. Read *MegaSkills* (Rich 1988). Select a few of the life skills for success on which to focus each month. Rich's book will give you ideas for teaching some of the concepts. Create award certificates for students who exhibit the Life Skills you are working on.

3. Consider planning just one learning celebration during the year as a culminating event to a unit. Invite parents and the community. Experience your own success, as well!

# Bibliography

**Works marked with asterisks are highly recommended.**

Apple, Michael W., and James A. Beane, eds. 1995. *Democratic Schools.* Alexandria, Va.: ASCD.

Armstrong, Thomas. 1994, 2000. *Multiple Intelligences in the Classroom.* Alexandria, Va.: ASCD.

———. 1993, 1999. *7 Kinds of Smart.* New York: Penguin.

Baratta-Lorton, Mary. 1976. *Mathematics Their Way.* Menlo Park, Calif.: Addison-Wesley.

Belvel, Patricia. 1998. Interview, December 1, San Jose, Calif.

———. 1995. *Twenty-First Century Classroom Leadership.* San Jose, Calif.: Training and Consulting Institute.

Brooks, Jacqueline Grennon, and Martin G. Brooks. 1993. *The Case for Constructivist Classrooms.* Alexandria, Va.: ASCD.

Caine, Geoffrey, Renate Nummela Caine, and Sam Crowell. 1999. *MindShifts: A Brain-Based Process for Restructuring Schools and Renewing Education.* Rev. Ed. Tucson, Ariz.: Zephyr Press.

*Caine, Renate Nummela, and Geoffrey Caine. 1994. *Making Connections: Teaching and the Human Brain.* Alexandria, Va.: ASCD.

———. 1997a. *Education on the Edge of Possibility.* Alexandria, Va.: ASCD.

———. 1997b. *Unleashing the Power of Perceptual Change.* Alexandria, Va.: ASCD.

Caplan, Jeff. 1998. Interview. December, Santa Cruz, Calif.

Checkley, Kathy. 1998. "No Room for Control." *Education Update* 40, 6: 4–7.

Crebbs, Stirling. 1999. *I Have a Choice* posters. Tucson, Ariz.: Zephyr Press.

*Csikszentmihalyi, Mihaly. 1990. *Flow: The Psychology of Optimal Experience.* New York: HarperCollins.

*DiGiulio, Robert. 1995. *Positive Classroom Management.* Thousand Oaks, Calif.: Corwin Press.

Dewey, John. 1916. *Democracy and Education.* New York: Macmillan.

Dickerson, Victoria. 1997. *If Problems Talked.* Cupertino, Calif.: Guilford Press.

*Elias, Michael J., Joseph E. Zins, Roger P. Weissberg, Karin S. Frey, Mark T. Greenberg, Morris M. Haynes, Rachael Kessler, Mary E. Schwab-Stone, and Timothy P. Shriver. 1997. *Promoting Social and Emotional Learning: Guidelines for Educators.* Alexandria, Va.: ASCD.

*Faber, Adele, and Elaine Mazlish. 1995. *How to Talk so Kids Can Learn.* New York: Rason.

———. 1980. *How to Talk so Kids Can Listen and Listen so Kids Can Talk.* New York: Avon.

Gardner, Howard. 1983. *Frames of Mind.* New York: Harper and Row.

*Gibbs, Jeanne. 1995. *Tribes: A New Way of Learning and Being Together.* Santa Rosa, Calif.: Center Source.

*Glasser, William. 1986. *Control Theory in the Classroom.* New York: Harper and Row.

Glenn, H. Stephen, and Jane Nelson. 1989. *Raising Self-Reliant Children in a Self-Indulgent World.* Rocklin, Calif.: Prime.

*Goleman, Daniel. 1994. *Emotional Intelligence: Why It Can Matter More than IQ.* New York: Bantam.

*Grant, Jim, Bob Johnson, and Irv Richardson. 1996. *Our Best Advice: The Multiage Problem Solving Handbook.* Peterborough, N.H.: Crystal Springs.

Hannaford, Carla. 1995. *Smart Moves.* Arlington, Va.: Great Ocean.

Harris, James M. 1989. *You and Your Child's Self-Esteem.* New York: Warner.

*Hart, Leslie. 1998. *Human Brain and Human Learning.* Rev. Ed. Kent, Wash.: Books for Educators.

*Healy, Jane. 1990. *Endangered Minds.* New York: Simon and Schuster.

———. 1987. *Your Child's Growing Mind.* New York: Doubleday.

*Jensen, Eric. 1996. *Brain-Based Learning.* Del Mar, Calif.: Turning Point.

———. 1997. *Completing the Brain-Compatible Puzzle.* 2d ed. Del Mar, Calif.: The Brain Store.

*———. 1998. *Teaching with the Brain in Mind.* Alexandria, Va.: ASCD.

Johnson, Spencer, and Constance Johnson. 1988. *The One-Minute Teacher.* New York: William and Morrow.

*Kohn, Alfie. 1996. *Beyond Discipline: From Compliance to Community.* Alexandria, Va.: ASCD.

———. 1993. *Punished by Rewards.* Boston, Mass.: Houghton Mifflin.

Kovalik, Susan. 1993. *ITI: The Model.* Kent, Wash.: Books for Educators.

Kunzler, Donna. 1998. *Brain Smart* posters. Tucson, Ariz.: Zephyr Press.

Lazear, David. 1999. *Eight Ways of Knowing: Teaching for Multiple Intelligences.* Arlington Heights, Ill.: Skylight.

———. 1994. *MI Approaches to Assessment: Solving the Assessment Conundrum.* Tucson, Ariz.: Zephyr Press.

———. 1997. *The Rubrics Way: Using MI to Assess Understanding.* Tucson, Ariz.: Zephyr Press.

Ledoux, Joseph. 1996. *The Emotional Brain: The Mysterious Underpinnings of Emotional Life.* New York: Touchstone.

Lewis, Barbara. 1991. *The Kid's Guide to Social Action.* Minneapolis, Minn.: Free Spirit.

Lickona, Thomas. 1991. *Educating for Character.* New York: Bantam.

Lowery, Lawrence. 1989. *Thinking and Learning: Matching Developmental Stages with Curriculum and Instruction.* Pacific Grove, Calif.: Midwest.

Margulies, Nancy. 1991. *Mapping Inner Space: Learning and Teaching Mind Mapping.* Tucson, Ariz.: Zephyr Press.

Margulies, Nancy, and Robert Sylwester. 1998. *Emotion and Attention.* Discover Your Brain series. Tucson, Ariz.: Zephyr Press.

Miller, Norma, ed. 1995. *The Healthy School Handbooks: Conquering the Sick Building Syndrome and Other Environmental Hazards in and around Your School.* Washington, D.C.: NEA.

Nelsen, Jane, and H. S. Glenn. 1993. *Positive Discipline in the Classroom.* Rocklin, Calif.: Prima.

Nelsen, Jane, and Lynn Lott. 1994. *Positive Discipline for Teenagers.* Rocklin, Calif.: Prima.

Ornstein, Robert. 1991. *The Evolution of Consciousness.* New York: Simon and Schuster.

Pert, Candace. 1997. *Molecules of Emotion: Why You Feel the Way You Feel.* New York: Scribner.

Politano, Colleen, and Joy Paquin. 2000. *Brain-Based Learning with Class.* Winnipeg, Manitoba: Portage & Main.

Porro, Barbara. 1996. *Talk It Out: Conflict Resolution in the Elementary Classroom.* Alexandria, Va.: ASCD.

Rich, Dorothy. 1988. *MegaSkills.* Boston, Mass.: Houghton Mifflin.

Slavin, Robert. 1994. *A Practical Guide to Cooperative Learning.* Boston, Mass.: Allyn and Bacon.

Smith, Frank. 1986. *Insult to Intelligence.* New York: Arbor House.

Stryker, Susan. 1983a. *The Anti-Coloring Book.* New York: Henry Holt.

———. 1983b. *The Anti-Coloring Book of Masterpieces.* New York: Henry Holt.

———. 1983c. *The Mystery Anti-Coloring Book.* New York: Henry Holt.

*Sylwester, Robert. 1995. *A Celebration of Neurons.* Alexandria, Va.: ASCD.

———. 1998. "The Downshifting Dilemma." Unpubl. paper.

Unell, Barbara, and Jerry Wycoff. 1995. *Twenty Teachable Virtues.* Berkeley, Calif.: Celestial Arts.

*Venolia, Carol. 1988. *Healing Environments.* Berkeley, Calif.: Celestial Arts.

*Wong, Harry, and Rosemary Tripi Wong. 1991. *The First Days of School.* Sunnyvale, Calif.: Wong.

# Index

# About the Author

Martha Kaufeldt has been an independent educational consultant, author, and keynote speaker for more than fifteen years. She presents dynamic workshops across the country on curriculum and instruction, school restructuring, multiage classrooms, and brain-based learning. Since 1977, Martha has worked as a teacher at all grade levels and has served as a district level gifted education coordinator and staff developer. She was a trainer for the Kovalik Integrated Thematic Instruction model for eight years. Most recently, she was lead teacher at Monarch Community School. Martha received a master's degree in human behavior from City University Extension in Seattle.

# It's Mind Boggling What Brain-Based Learning Can Do for Your Students!

## BRAINDEMONIUM

Illustrations by Adam Gilbert

*Grades 7–12*

Let your students in on the party! Each person's brain is a gift to celebrate. Share with your students the value and importance of brain function and anatomy through eight thought-provoking posters. Topics include—

- Your Brain
- Brain Lobes
- Neurons
- Train Your Brain
- Brain Healthy
- And more!

*8 full-color, 11" x 17" posters*

**1120-W . . . $27**

## BRAIN FOOD

*Games That Make Kids Think*

by Paul Fleisher, M.Ed.

*Grades 4–12+*

Be the one to make a difference in your students' thinking! With more than 100 games to choose from, *Brain Food* is your one-stop source for exploring the fun in learning. This compilation is filled with new as well as traditional games, and most need little more than paper and pencil to get you started. Each game is classroom tested and tailored to enhance the intelligences of your students. You'll find—

- 70 reproducible game boards
- More than 100 word, logical, mathematical, and strategic games
- A multicultural selection of games from places as varied as Africa, Denmark, New Zealand, and Indonesia

**1088-W . . . $36**

— — — — **Buy these and other brain-based learning resources at www.zephyrpress.com** — — — —

| Qty. | Item # | Title | Unit Price | Total |
|------|--------|-------|-----------|-------|
| | 1120-W | Braindemonium posters (set of 8) | $27 | |
| | 1088-W | Brain Food | $36 | |
| | | | | |
| | | | | |

Name _____

Address _____

City _____

State _____ Zip _____

Phone (_____) _____

E-mail _____

**Method of payment (check one):**

❑ Check or Money Order   ❑ Visa

❑ MasterCard   ❑ Purchase Order Attached

Credit Card No. _____

Expires _____

Signature _____

| | |
|---|---|
| Subtotal | |
| Sales Tax (AZ residents, 5%) | |
| S & H (10% of subtotal–min $4.00) | |
| Total (U.S. funds only) | |

CANADA: add 22% for S & H and G.S.T.

**100% SATISFACTION GUARANTEE**

If at any time, for any reason, you're not completely satisfied with your purchase, return your order in saleable condition for a 100% refund (excluding shipping and handling). No questions asked!

**Call, Write, or FAX for your FREE Catalog!**

## Zephyr Press ®

REACHING THEIR HIGHEST POTENTIAL

P.O. Box 66006-W
Tucson, AZ 85728-6006

520-322-5090
1-800-232-2187
FAX 520-323-9402

Please include your phone number in case we have questions about your order.